*Law*Basics

PROPERTY

FIRST EDITION

*Law*Basics

PROPERTY

FIRST EDITION

By

David A. Brand, LL.B. (Hons), W.S., Solicitor

Senior Lecturer in Law and Director of the Diploma in Legal Practice, University of Dundee

W. GREEN

 **THOMSON REUTERS**

Published in 2009 by Thomson Reuters (Legal) Limited
(Registered in England & Wales, Company No 1679046.
Registered Office and address for service:
100 Avenue Road, London NW3 3PF
trading as W. Green)

Typeset by Keith Thaxton at W. Green, Edinburgh
Printed and bound in Great Britain by Athenaeum Press Ltd, Gateshead.

No natural forests were destroyed to make this product;
only farmed timber was used and re-planted.

A CIP catalogue record for this book is available from the British
Library.

ISBN 978 0 414 017641

Thomson Reuters and the Thomson Reuters logo are
trademarks of Thomson Reuters.

CONTENTS

Page

Table of Cases vii

1. Introduction and General Concepts 1
2. Corporeal Moveable Property 10
3. Incorporeal Moveable Property 17
4. Rights in Security over Moveable Property 20
5. Landownership 24
6. Restrictions on Landownership 46
7. Leases 63
8. Securities over Heritable Property 73
9. Conveyancing and a Typical Conveyancing Transaction 80

Bibliography 91
Index 93

CONTENTS

TABLE OF CASES

Page

ABERDEEN CITY COUNCIL V WANCHOO [2008] CSIH 6; 2008 S.C. 278; 2008 S.L.T. 106 60
Aberdeen College Board of Management v Youngson [2005] CSOH 31;
    2005 1 S.C. 335; 2005 S.L.T. 371...31
Aberdeen Varieties Ltd v James F Donald (Aberdeen Cinemas) Ltd,
    1940 S.C. (H.L.) 52; 1940 S.L.T. 374...52
Anderson v Dickie, 1915 S.C. (H.L.) 79; (1915) 1 S.L.T.393 52
—— v Valentine, 1985 S.C.C.C. 89...11
Angus v National Coal Board, 1955 S.C. 175; 1955 S.L.T. 245...43
Armour v Thyssen Edelstahlwerke AG [1991] 2 A.C. 339; [1990] 3 W.L.R. 810...............16
Assessor for Fife v Hodgson, 1966 S.C. 30; 1966 S.L.T. 79 34

BAIN V BRAND (1875-76) L.R. 1 App. Cas. 762; (1876) 3 R. (H.L.) 16 ....34, 35
Ballantyne v Meoni, 1997 G.W.D. 29-1489..66
Barker v Lewis, 2008 S.L.T. (Sh Ct) 17; 2008 G.W.D. 9-167 55
Bayley v Addison (1801) 8 S.L.T. 379...67
Ben Challum Ltd v Buchanan, 1955 S.C. 348; 1955 S.L.T. 294 56
Blair Trust Co v Gilbert, 1940 S.L.T. 322..66
Bowers v Kennedy, 2000 S.C. 555; 2000 S.L.T. 1006...59
Brand's Trustees v Brand's Trustees. *See* Bain v Brand
Burnett's Trustee v Grainger [2004] UKHL 8; 2004 S.C. (H.L.) 19;
    2004 S.L.T. 513...30, 83

CALEDONIAN RAILWAY CO V SPROT (1856) 2 Macq. 449 43
Cantor Properties (Scotland) Ltd v Swears and Wells Ltd, 1980 S.L.T. 165.......................69
Chevron Petroleum (UK) Ltd v Post Office, 1986 S.C. 291; 1987 S.L.T. 588...................66
Christie v Smith, 1949 S.C. 572; 1950 S.L.T. 31 ....5, 34
Clark v West Calder Oil Co (1882) 9 R. 1017 15
Cochrane v Stevenson (1891) 18 R. 1208..34
Crown Estate Commissioners v Fairlie Yacht Slip Ltd, 1979 S.C. 156 44
Cumbernauld and Kilsyth DC v Dollar Land (Cumbernauld) Ltd,
    1993 S.C. (H.L.) 44; 1993 S.L.T. 1318...61

DAVID WATSON PROPERTY MANAGEMENT V WOOLWICH EQUITABLE BUILDING SOCIETY,
    1992 S.C. (H.L.) 21; 1992 S.L.T. 430...77
Deans v Woolfson, 1922 S.C. 221; 1922 S.L.T. 165...8
Dick v Clydesdale Bank Plc, 1991 S.C. 365; 1991 S.L.T. 678 77

EWART V COCHRANE (1869) 4 Macq. 117 59

FRY'S METALS LTD V DURASTIC LTD, 1991 S.L.T. 689 67

GLENDINNING V HOPE & CO. *See* John D Hope & Co v Glendinning
Gloag v Perth and Kinross Council, 2007 S.C.L.R. 530...42
Golden Sea Produce Ltd v Scottish Nuclear Plc, 1992 S.L.T. 942 65
Gray v Edinburgh University, 1962 S.C. 157; 1962 S.L.T. 173..64
Gunn v National Coal Board, 1982 S.L.T. 526 66

HALKERSTON V WEDDERBURN (1781) Mor. 10495..32
Hay's Trustees v Young (1877) 4 R. 398..41
Hayman & Son v McLintock; sub nom. Hayman & Son v M'lintock & Others,
    1907 S.C. 936; (1907) 15 S.L.T. 63..16
Hislop v MacRitchie's Trustees (1881) 8 R. (H.L.) 95 54

INGLIS V ROBERTSON; sub nom. Irvine v Inglis; Irvine & Robertson v Baxter & Inglis
    [1898] A.C. 616; (1898) 6 S.L.T. 130..16

International Banking Corp v Ferguson Shaw & Sons, 1910 S.C. 182;
 1909 2 S.L.T. 377 14

JA Pye (Oxford) Ltd v United Kingdom (44302/02) (2006) 43 E.H.R.R. 3;
 19 B.H.R.C. 705, ECHR 32
John D Hope & Co v Glendinning; sub nom. Glendinning v Hope & Co;
 Glendinning v John D Hope & Co [1911] A.C. 419; 1911 S.C. (H.L.) 73 22

Kildrummy (Jersey) Ltd v Inland Revenue Commissioners [1990] S.T.C. 657;
 1991 S.C. 1 64
Kippen v Oppenheim (1847) 10 D. 242 66

Lamb v Grant (1874) 11 S.L.R. 672 ....5, 16
Lord Advocate v Aberdeen University, 1963 S.C. 533; 1963 S.L.T. 361 13
—— v Reo Stakis Organisation Ltd; sub nom. Secretary of State for the Environment v
 Reo Stakis Organisation Ltd, 1981 S.C. 104; 1982 S.L.T. 140 43
Lousada & Co Ltd v JE Lesser (Properties) Ltd, 1990 S.C. 178; 1990 S.L.T. 823 68

Mackenzie v MacLean (George Malcolm), 1981 S.L.T. (Sh. Ct.) 40 12
McDonald v Provan (Of Scotland Street) Ltd, 1960 S.L.T. 231 14
Mactaggart & Co v Harrower (1906) 8 F. 1101; (1906) 14 S.L.T. 277 54
Malloch v McLean (1867) 5 M. 335 5
Mendelssohn v The Wee Pub Co Ltd, 1991 G.W.D. 26-1518 58
Mickel v McCoard, 1913 S.C. 1036; 1913 2 S.L.T. 106 67
Milton v Glen-Moray Distillery Co Ltd; sub nom. Milton v Glen Moray
 Glenlivet Distillery Co Ltd (1898) 1 F. 135; (1898) 6 S.L.T. 206 44
—— v Glen Moray Glenlivet Distillery Co Ltd. *See* Milton v Glen-Moray
 Distillery Co Ltd
Moncrieff v Jamieson [2007] UKHL 42; [2007] 1 W.L.R. 2620; [2008] 4 All E.R. 752 58
Montgomerie v Buchanan's Trustees (1853) 15 D. 853 44
More v Boyle, 1967 S.L.T. (Sh. Ct.) 38 48
Murray v Dunn; sub nom. Murray's Trustees v St Margaret's Convent's Trustees;
 Murray's Trustees v Trustees for St Margaret's Convent [1907] A.C. 283;
 1907 S.C. (H.L.) 8 52
—— v Medley, 1973 S.L.T. (Sh. Ct.) 75 59
Murray's Trustees v St Margaret's Convent's Trustees. *See* Murray v Dunn

Neill v Scobbie, 1993 G.W.D. 13-887 58
North British Railway Co v Turners Ltd (1904) 6 F. 900;
 (1904) 12 S.L.T. 176 43
North West Securities Ltd v Barrhead Coachworks Ltd, 1976 S.C. 68;
 1976 S.L.T. 99 16

Orr Ewing & Co v Colquhoun's Trustees (1873) 4 R. (H.L.) 116 44

Pacitti v Manganiello, 1995 S.C.L.R. 557 68
Prangnell-O'Neill v Lady Skiffington, 1984 S.L.T. 282 6

RHM Bakeries (Scotland) Ltd v Strathclyde RC, 1985 S.C. (H.L.) 17;
 1985 S.L.T. 214 48
Rafique v Amin, 1997 S.L.T. 1385; 1997 G.W.D. 3-118 ....8, 37
Redfearn v Somervail (1830) 1 Dow 50 18
Renfrew DC v Gray, 1987 S.L.T. (Sh. Ct.) 70 68
Retail Parks Investments Ltd v Royal Bank of Scotland Plc (No.2), 1996 S.C. 227;
 1996 S.L.T. 669 66
Ross v Baird (1827) 7 S. 361 48

Safeway Stores Plc v Tesco Stores Ltd; sub nom. Tesco Stores Ltd v Keeper of the
 Registers of Scotland, 2004 S.C. 29; 2004 S.L.T. 701 28
Scottish Discount Co Ltd v Blin, 1985 S.C. 216; 1986 S.L.T. 123 35

Scottish Widows Fund v Buist (1876) 3 R. 1078..15, 17
Sharp v Thomson; sub nom. Sharp v Woolwich Building Society;
    Sharp v Joint Receivers of Albyn Construction Ltd, 1997 S.C. (H.L.) 66;
    1997 S.L.T. 636..29, 30, 83
Smith v Bank of Scotland; Mumford v Bank of Scotland, 1997 S.C. (H.L.) 111;
    1997 S.L.T. 1061...78
Snowie v Stirling Council, 2008 S.L.T. (Sh Ct) 61; 2008 Hous. L.R. 46 43
Spyer v Phillipson [1931] 2 Ch. 183 35
Sunbolf v Alford (1838) 2 M. & W. 248 23
Syme v Harvey (1861) 24 D. 202 35

Tailors of Aberdeen v Coutts (1870) 1 Rob. App. 296 51
Tuley v Highland Council, 2009 G.W.D. 18-292; 2009 S.L.T. 616......................................43

Upper Crathes Fishings Ltd v Bailey's Executors; sub nom. Upper Crathes
    Fishings Ltd v Barclay, 1991 S.C. 30; 1991 S.L.T. 747 8

Walker v Whitwell, 1916 S.C. (H.L.) 75; 1916 1 S.L.T. 2...84
Webster v Lord Advocate, 1985 S.C. 173; 1985 S.L.T. 361 48
West Lothian Oil Co Ltd v Mair (1892) 20 R. 64 15
Wills Trustees v Cairngorm Canoeing & Sailing School Ltd, 1976 S.C. (H.L.) 30;
    1976 S.L.T. 162..44
Winans v Macrae (1885) 12 R. 1051..41
Wood v North British Railway Co (1899) 1 F. 562; (1899) 6 S.L.T. 323 41

Young & Co v Bankier Distillery Co (1893) 20 R. (H.L.) 76 44

1. INTRODUCTION AND GENERAL CONCEPTS

INTRODUCTION

Property law in Scotland is an extensive area of law, as in all legal systems. It covers various rights and obligations in relation to what is generally termed property. This includes land, moveable items and intangible items such as intellectual property. Property law deals with the creation, transfer and extinction of such rights and obligations. Everyone is affected by property law. All people own some property, whether it is a substantial house, a bank account, the right to proceeds of an insurance company or simply the clothes they are wearing and not much else. People who do not own their homes and rent from a landlord have a tenancy under a lease, which is a type of property right. Everyone has the right to cross substantial parts of the Scottish countryside. This is a public right and directly affects the property rights of many landowners, as it restricts the use they can make of their own land.

Property law in Scotland is very distinctive. It is quite different from the law in England in most respects and much of it is based on Roman law from which many areas of Scots law derive. This is particularly true of moveable property. Certain areas of property law in the commercial field, such as sale of goods, have been influenced by English law. The law in these areas is the same as or similar to that in England and has moved away from Roman law principles, although many of these underlying principles remain. Other specific areas, notably intellectual property, are governed by UK wide statutes, but our system of property law remains largely our own.

As with most European countries, property law which deals with land has been largely influenced by feudal principles. The feudal system continued to operate in Scotland, albeit in limited form, until very recently. The fundamental principle of feudalism was that land was not owned outright and all land derived from the Crown. This system, which originated in continental Europe, was introduced into Scotland back in the twelfth century. The system was originally very effective, but over the centuries was modernised and reformed. Strict feudal principles were diluted until it was finally abolished in 2004 after devolution.

The law itself is based on both statutory and common law sources. Unlike some other jurisdictions based on Roman law to a greater or lesser extent, there is no codification of the law. Neither is there any general consolidating statute relating to property law. Instead, the statutes are spread over a long period of time dating as far back as the Royal Mines Act 1424 and the Leases Act 1449. Added to these diverse statutes is an extensive amount of common law which has developed over the centuries. This results in a large and varied amount of primary sources which must be studied to gain a comprehensive knowledge of Scottish property law.

One area which has been subject to a significant amount of recent legislative activity is land law. Substantial reform of land law has taken place since devolution, which has effectively modernised a major part of property law. When the Scottish Parliament was established after devolution, the first Scottish Executive chose land law reform, and the abolition of the feudal system in particular, as one of its key reforms to symbolise a new, modern Scotland. Accordingly, an extensive programme of land reform legislation was undertaken following a series of Reports by the Scottish Law Commission. This led to, amongst other matters, the abolition of the feudal system under the Abolition of Feudal Tenure etc. (Scotland) Act 2000, reform of real burdens, which are restrictions on the use of land, under the Title Conditions (Scotland) Act 2003, the "right to roam" under the Land Reform (Scotland) Act 2003 and reform of tenement law under the Tenements (Scotland) Act 2004. All these will be examined in the following chapters.

In this modern world of human rights, Scottish property law is affected by human rights legislation, as one would expect. Under the Scotland Act 1998, a breach of the rights under the European Convention on Human Rights may be challenged. The Convention did not originally include property law, but this was added by Protocol 1 art.1. This provides that people are entitled to peaceful enjoyment of their possessions and no-one shall be deprived of his or her possessions except in the public interest. It preserves the right of a state to enforce laws necessary to control property in the general interest. The effect of this has not been extensive, but Convention rights have been considered by the courts in a number of areas, including real burdens and prescription.

This book aims to give an account of the basic principles of Scottish property law. Such an account cannot be completely comprehensive and there are limitations on the amount of detail which can be included. It does not include the law relating to succession or trusts, which can be regarded as either separate topics or significant parts of property law. Although conveyancing is not included, there is a final chapter giving a brief outline of a typical conveyancing transaction and covering certain aspects of conveyancing. A bibliography is provided for further reading.

GENERAL CONCEPTS

In order to understand property law, there are various general concepts which must be comprehended at the outset. These are fundamental and the details of the law cannot be understood without knowledge of these.

What is Property?

What exactly do we mean by the term "property"? Most people understand this to mean actual physical items such as a house, a car or an iPod. In this sense, property means the actual thing which is owned. This need not be tangible, as a credit balance in a bank account or the proceeds of a life policy are obviously items of property. Shares in a company are another example of property. This is property, although it is not a physical, tangible item which can be touched. Such property is said to be incorporeal property.

The term "property" can also be used to signify the right of ownership of something or some less extensive right than outright ownership. If I own the house where I live, I have a property right in the house. This is the property right of ownership. If there is a mortgage over the house, the lender of the mortgage will have a security over the house, which is a lesser property right. If I let my house to a tenant, the tenant will have a lease of the house. This is also a property right. It is clear from these examples that there are different types of property right and that it is possible for more than one property right to exist in the same thing or item of property.

Ownership and lesser property rights

As we have now seen, the term property can be used in two different ways, referring either to the actual rights in a thing or the thing itself. The most complete property right is ownership. Property in this sense is known as *dominium* in Roman law. Property in the second sense of the thing owned is known as a *res* in Roman law.

The classic definition of property in the sense of ownership in Scots law is given by Erskine. He states that it is:

> "the right of using and disposing of a subject as our own, except in so far as we are restrained by law or paction [agreement]".[1]

The first part of this definition states what most people understand as property. The owner can do whatever he or she wants with the item or subject. The owner can enjoy it, alter it, give it away or sell it. The second part qualifies this by making it clear that this right is not absolute. The law imposes restrictions on the exercise of the right of ownership and the owner may agree to restrict the right. For instance, an owner cannot use the subject in a way which causes a nuisance to neighbours or for a purpose which requires planning permission. These are restrictions on absolute ownership which the common law or specific statutes impose on an owner. In addition, an owner may agree to a restriction on the absolute use of the subject, for instance, by granting a neighbour a servitude right of access over the subject.

If a person owns property, the rights which ownership confers are extensive, although not unlimited. They are sometimes referred to as a bundle of rights. They are known as *jura in re propria,* rights in a property which a person owns. Other property rights which are less extensive than ownership are usually referred to as subordinate rights. As these rights are lesser rights than ownership, they relate to property which someone else owns. They are known as *jura in re aliena.* Examples of these include:

- rights of tenants in leased property;
- rights of a creditor where the property has been used as a security;
- servitude rights such as a right of way over a neighbour's property; and
- the rights of beneficiaries under a trust.

Classification of property

Property can be classified in various ways according to its nature. These are:

* heritable and moveable;
* corporeal and incorporeal; and
* fungible and non-fungible.

Classification within these categories is important because various property rules relating to transfer, rights in security and succession depend on how a property is classified. There are different rules on these matters for different types of property.

Heritable and moveable

The most important classification is whether a property is heritable or moveable. All property will be one or the other. Most heritable property is classified as heritable because of its nature, and broadly covers land and buildings or anything attached to the land. Rights connected with land and buildings, such as servitudes and leases, are also heritable. All other property is moveable, which is by its nature capable of being moved, such as furniture and cars. Rights connected with moveables, such as a right to sue under contract or delict, are also moveable rights.

This classification of property into heritable or moveable derives from the old law of intestate succession in Scots law, which had different rules on who would succeed to the property of a deceased where there was no will. Under the ancient principle of *primogeniture,* the land or heritable property went to the heir-at-law who was the eldest son. This rule from a different social era was abolished by the Succession (Scotland) Act 1964.

The distinction between heritable and moveable property still remains important in relation to legal rights in succession to property on death. Legal rights exist under Scots law to prevent people from completely disinheriting their closest relatives. They can be claimed by a spouse or registered civil partner and the children of someone who has died, regardless of whether the deceased has made a will or not. These rights are only available from the moveable part of the property of the deceased. They do not apply to the deceased's heritable property. This distinction may be abolished as part of reform of the law of succession which is currently under review.

Some types of property are clearly heritable or moveable. Land and buildings are obviously heritable, as are trees. When trees are cut down as timber, the timber is clearly moveable. Cows grazing in a field are obviously moveable. The grass on which the cows are grazing is growing out of the ground and is acceding to, or attached to, the soil. Natural fruits of the land which require no constant cultivation, including grass, are regarded as heritable by nature and remain so until severed from the land.[2] An exception to this rule is made in relation to what are known as industrial growing crops. These are classified as moveable although physically growing from the soil and acceding to the land. These crops, such as barley, wheat, and potatoes, require cultivation and are classified as moveable.[3]

This principle of property law where something growing accedes to where it grows is known as accession by fruits. The examples of trees and grass relate to heritable property, but the principle also applies to growing things in moveable property. Young unborn animals accede to their mothers.[4]

So far, the classification between heritable and moveable property is straightforward due to the nature of the property. The classification can become more complicated because property may become heritable, not by its nature, but by accession or by destination. Accession is where property which is originally moveable converts to heritable property by attachment to the land. Destination is where certain moveable property is treated as heritable in cases of succession.

Accession will occur in such circumstances as where a substantial summerhouse is erected on land and becomes part of that land,[5] or where a fireplace is built into a room in a building on land. What was originally moveable converts to being heritable under the principle of accession. The question of whether a moveable item has converted to become a heritable item can be a difficult one and is a problem area in the sale and purchase of houses and other heritable properties. It is generally known as the law of fixtures and is discussed more fully below.

In succession, there is the possibility that certain moveable property may be classified as heritable by destination. This means that certain moveable items are regarded as heritable because that was the implied intention of the deceased. This has limited operation. In an old case,[6] a person died during the construction of a building and the materials to be used in the construction were regarded as heritable for the purpose of succession to the deceased's estate.

Corporeal and incorporeal

Property is corporeal if it is tangible and can be seen or touched, such as furniture or jewellery. Incorporeal property is intangible and includes such items as shares in a company or an insurance policy. A share certificate or insurance policy document is tangible and corporeal, but the right itself is intangible and incorporeal. These examples are moveable but both heritable and moveable property can be either corporeal or incorporeal. Land is corporeal heritable property and rights relating to land, such as a lease or a servitude, are incorporeal heritable property.

Fungible and non-fungible

A fungible property is property which disappears when used but can be replaced by a similar property, such as milk or money. A non-fungible property is one which cannot be replaced readily and has an inherent value, such as a work of art. In other words, fungible property is non-specific, whereas non-fungible property is specific.

Ownership and possession

Possession is an important concept in both heritable and moveable property. One of the incidents of unrestricted ownership is the right to exclusive possession and the ability to prevent others from interfering with it. An owner of land is entitled to be free from persons trespassing or encroaching on the land, although there are now extensive rights of access to land, discussed below. In land law, the operation of prescription is fundamental. This is the principle whereby land held on a good title and possessed for the appropriate period of time, usually ten years, is free from challenge by anyone claiming title to that land. Possession is also important in moveable property. There is a presumption that the possessor of goods is the owner, in the absence of evidence to the contrary.[7] This gives some weight to the popular phrase, "possession is nine tenths of the law". It is a presumption only but is difficult to rebut.

Possession can be either natural or civil.[8] Natural possession is where the possessor actually occupies the land or retains the goods personally. Civil is where the possession is by another on behalf of the owner. If a person owns a house and actually lives there, this is natural possession by the owner. If the owner leases the house to a tenant and the tenant lives there, this is civil possession by the tenant.

What constitutes possession itself may not be straightforward. The classic definition states:

> "there must be an act of the body which is the detention and holding; and an act of the mind which is the inclination or affection to make use of the thing obtained".[9]

This means that there are two elements which are an act of body, meaning there must be a physical element of actual retention and holding the property, plus an act of mind, meaning the mental intention to possess property for oneself.[10]

It is possible to have one element without the other. A person can have actual physical retention of the property without intending to keep it as his or her own. The property may be held on behalf of someone else, such as a friend or employer, and in this case there is no legal possession, only custody. It is also possible to have possession of the property without a legal right, as where a thief is in possession of stolen goods intending to keep them and satisfies both elements of possession.

A thief is a good example of someone who has possession unlawfully. It is possible to be a lawful possessor or an unlawful possessor. A squatter is an example of someone who is an unlawful possessor of land. An unlawful possessor has no right to the property despite having possession. It is also possible to be a possessor without a right to be in good faith or bad faith. A thief or a squatter is a possessor in bad faith. If someone possesses property without a right to it, but honestly believes that he or she did have a right, that person will be a possessor in good faith, or *bona fide*. This might arise if someone honestly, but mistakenly, believes that he or she had been gifted an item of property. If a possessor in good faith makes any improvements to the property, that person will be entitled to compensation when possession is given up. There will also be an entitlement to any fruits of the property, for example, any natural produce produced by the land.

Where the owner of property has lost possession and seeks to recover this, there are various actions open to the owner including raising an action for restitution and the old common law remedy known as spuilzie, which is now rarely used.

Real rights and personal rights

There is an important fundamental distinction in property rights between real rights and personal rights. A real right is enforceable against anyone at all, whereas a personal right is enforceable only against a particular person or persons. Personal rights are created by an agreement or contract between the parties. Many types of personal rights and corresponding obligations can arise from the contract. These will be enforceable by the parties to the contract against each other, but not against third parties. A real right is enforceable against any third party who challenges its existence.

To take the example of a sale of a house, when houses are sold and transferred to the seller, the first stage is usually the missives. These are letters which constitute the contract for the sale and purchase of the house. When the missives are completed, there are several steps required before the house transfers to the seller and the seller becomes the owner. In the meantime, there is a completed enforceable contract. At this stage, the purchaser remains the owner. The seller could sell to someone else and transfer ownership to that person. The purchaser would then have to sue the seller for breach of contract. This would be on the basis of the personal right under the missives. Once all the steps to transfer ownership have been completed and the document transferring the title to the purchaser has been registered in the appropriate Register, the purchaser becomes the new owner and obtains a real right to defend that right of ownership against anyone.

Real rights are created in different ways for different types of property. Normally this involves two stages. The first stage will be an agreement or contract between the parties. In the case of the house, as it is heritable property, this is the missives stage when the contract for the sale and purchase is concluded. This gives rise to a personal right only. The next stage is a public act by registering the document of transfer of title in the appropriate public property register, either the Register of Sasines or the Land Register. This second stage of recording in the public property register creates the real right. This second stage can be viewed as an external act, which is necessary as it affects third parties who are not involved in the sale and purchase but who are given notice that it has taken place. It is usually referred to as the publicity principle.

There is also normally a two stage process with moveable property. In the transfer of corporeal moveables, the first stage is the agreement or contract between the parties and the second stage which creates the real right is the delivery of the moveables.

Co-ownership

Both heritable and moveable property can be owned by more than one person. There is a distinction between joint property, common property and common interest. Joint property and common property are types of co-ownership, which is also known as *pro indiviso* ownership, and the owners are said to have a *pro indiviso* share of ownership. Common interest relates to rights in a property owned by another person.

Joint property
This is where two or more persons own a property as an individual whole. The joint owner cannot dispose of the right of ownership during lifetime or, on death, by a will. When the ownership is surrendered or the person dies, that right of ownership accresces, or is added to, the other joint owner or owners. One example of this type of ownership is an unincorporated association, such as a club, where the members of the club own the club's property jointly and each club member will be a joint owner, but will cease to be so on ceasing to be a member. Another is trust property, where the trustees own trust property jointly. It is unusual for a number of individuals who do not have a common connection, such as a club, to hold property in this way.

Common property
Common property is much more widespread than joint property. This is where two or more persons own a property and each owner has an individual share of the property. This can be disposed of during the co-owner's lifetime or under a will or according to the rules of intestate succession on death. A co-owner can also divide his or her share or grant a security over it. If a co-owner wishes to dispose of his or her share and the other co-owner or co-owners refuse, it is open to apply to the court, in an action of division and sale, to have the court order that the whole property be sold and the proceeds divided amongst the co-owners.[11]

The usual example of co-ownership is a husband and wife or other couple owning their home as common property. It is usually said that their title is in joint names, but this is confusing and does not mean that the property is joint property. If the property is owned in common by a married couple and one spouse wishes to sell and the other does not, there are protection provisions in actions of sale and division.[12]

The general rule for management of common property is that all co-owners must consent to the management of the property. This includes any alterations, improvements or repairs to the property.[13] This means one co-owner can veto the proposals of all the others. In the case of essential repairs, it is possible for one co-owner to instruct these and recover the appropriate share of the cost from the other co-owners.[14] In relation to tenements, parts of which are common property, the rules on repairs to common property were a problem area prior to the introduction of statutory rules under the Tenements (Scotland) Act 2004. These are considered in the section on the law of the tenement below.

Common interest

Common interest is not a right of ownership, but is an important right in relation to property owned by another. It is a right which an owner of property has in respect of property owned by another by implication of law. This right acts as a restriction on what the owner of the property can do with the property as certain actions may affect the property of the other person.

In a tenement building, in the absence of provision in the title deeds, a ground floor flat owner will own the section of the external gable wall enclosing the flat. An upper floor flat owner does not have an ownership right in respect of that section of the gable wall, but does have a right of common interest in that section. This is because the whole wall, including the section owned by the ground floor owner, supports all the flats in the tenement, including the upper flat. The ground floor flat owner cannot do anything which adversely affects the right of common interest of support, such as putting in a new window which destabilises the gable wall. This common law position was re-enforced under the 2004 Act.

Common interest occurs mainly in the law of the tenement, but can occur in other situations, such as where owners of a river have a common interest in the water of the river.

Other types of property right

Liferents

A liferent is a special type of property right. It is the right to the use of or income from a property during the lifetime of the person who has the right, known as the liferenter, or some other period set out in the deed constituting the liferent. It applies to both heritable and moveable property. The liferenter is not entitled to the capital of the property, known as the fee, which belongs to the person known as the fiar. The fiar is the owner of the property but will not have complete ownership of the property until the liferent comes to an end. During the liferent, the liferenter must not do anything to the detriment of the capital of the liferented subjects. Liferents are classed as either proper or improper liferents and alimentary liferents are an important type of improper liferent.

Occupancy rights of a non-entitled spouse

A new type of property right was introduced under the Matrimonial Homes (Family Protection) (Scotland) Act 1981. This is an occupancy right in relation to a matrimonial home. This is intended to give protection to either a husband or wife in the situation where only one of the married couple owns the home in which they live. If the couple own the home in common, each has a right of ownership which automatically gives the right to occupy or possess the home. If only one of them is the owner, prior to the Act there was nothing to prevent the owner evicting his wife or her husband. The Act was introduced to give married couples an equal right to occupy the home, regardless of who is the owner.

Under the Act, the owner is referred to as the entitled spouse and the non-owner as the non-entitled spouse. A non-entitled spouse is given occupancy rights which allow the spouse to continue to reside in the home and to re-enter and reside in the home if he or she is not living there. This is a property right which is enforceable under the Act.

The Act gives occupancy rights automatically to spouses and this was extended to registered civil partners by the Civil Partnership Act 2004. Under the 1981 Act, occupancy rights are not automatically given where a couple are cohabiting in a home and are not married, but provision is made for application to the court to obtain occupancy rights.

---

[1] Erskine, *Institute*. II, ii, 1.
[2] Erskine, *Institute*. II, ii, 3.
[3] Erskine, *Institute*. II, ii, 4.
[4] *Lamb v Grant* (1874) 11 S.L.R. 672.
[5] *Christie v Smith's Exr*, 1949 S.C. 572.
[6] *Malloch v McLean* (1867) 5 M. 335.
[7] Stair, II, i, 42, *Prangnell-O'Neill v Skiffington*, 1984 S.L.T. 282.
[8] Erskine, *Institute*. II, ii, 22.
[9] Stair, II, i, 17.
[10] This concept is known as *animus possidendi*.
[11] *Upper Crathes Fishings Ltd v Bailey's Exrs.*, 1991 S.L.T. 747.
[12] Matrimonial Homes (Family Protection) (Scotland) Act 1981 s.19.
[13] *Rafique v Amin*, 1997 S.L.T. 1385.
[14] *Deans v Woolfson*, 1922 S.C. 221.

---

2. CORPOREAL MOVEABLE PROPERTY

As we have seen, corporeal moveable property is tangible property which is capable of being moved. This chapter deals with how ownership of this type of property can be acquired and transferred.

Acquisition

Corporeal moveable property can be acquired in one of two ways. These are original acquisition and derivative acquisition. Original acquisition is where an item of property has never had an owner before it is acquired, or the owner has lost the right of ownership. It also includes property which is newly created and did not previously exist. Derivative acquisition is where the acquisition is by transfer from the existing owner to a new owner. There are different rules for each type of acquisition.

Original Acquisition

Original acquisition can be divided into four categories. These are:

- occupation;
- accession;
- specification; and
- confusion and commixtion.

Occupation
Corporeal moveable property which has never been owned by anyone becomes the property of the person who acquires it with the intention of becoming the owner.[15] This rule derives from the Roman law principle, *quod nullius est fit primi occupantis*, which means that what belongs to no-one becomes the property of the first taker. In reality, there is not much ownerless property available to be acquired by occupation. Most items of corporeal moveable property are owned by someone, but some items are not, such as pebbles or shells on a beach or wild animals, birds or fish. It may be possible to acquire these by occupation. Such property is known as *res nullius*. If I am in the woods and I see and capture a wild rabbit, I will become the owner of the rabbit. I can take it home and keep it as my own property.

There are various qualifications to this general rule of acquisition by occupation. Certain wild creatures cannot be acquired in this way, such as salmon and royal birds which belong to the Crown, or protected species, such as ospreys or badgers.[16] There are various statutory provisions to protect a large variety of wild animals, principally in the Wildlife and Countryside Act 1981.

In order to acquire property by occupation, there usually must be some degree of confinement to show the intention of becoming the owner. If the rabbit I captured in the woods escapes from me on my way home and disappears back into the woods, it is no longer my property and becomes a *res nullius* again. It is available for someone else to acquire as a wild animal. In contrast, if deer are captured and placed in a fenced compound, they remain the property of the taker and it is not possible to enter the compound and remove them to acquire ownership. Such removal would constitute theft. Some creatures, such as bees and pigeons, have a homing instinct and require little or no confinement.

Even if such confined wild creatures escape from their enclosure, some time may be allowed for these to be recaptured before these can be considered as *res nullius* again and available to be acquired by occupation. In *Anderson v Valentine*, 1985 S.C.C.R. 89, rainbow trout escaped from a fish farm and were caught by the accused in the vicinity of the enclosure from which they had escaped. The fish were held to remain the property of the fish farm and the accused were guilty of theft.

It is also the case that if a domestic animal escapes from confinement and is in the wild, it cannot be acquired by occupation and remains the property of the owner. If the owner continues to regard the animal as his or her property and wishes to recover possession of the animal, ownership of the animal is retained. If the owner gives up ownership by abandoning the animal, the animal does not become a *res nullius* but will belong to the Crown. It was suggested in *Anderson v Valentine* that if rainbow trout escaped into the wild they would not become *res nullius* as rainbow trout is not a wild species in Scotland. If they had ceased to belong to the fish farm owner by escaping further away from their enclosure, they would belong to the Crown .

Wild creatures which are not confined cannot be stolen. This may seem puzzling in relation to game or fish. The right to hunt for these usually belongs to the owner of the land on which they are found and this would seem to suggest that anyone is entitled to poach animals or fish on land belonging to someone else. The strict legal position is that a poacher can become the owner of wild animals or fish taken from someone's land under the principle of occupation, but poaching is a crime and there are statutory provisions which authorise forfeiture of the captured animals or fish on a conviction for poaching, such as the Night Poaching Act 1828.

Property which is either lost or abandoned cannot be acquired by occupation. Lost property is not the same as abandoned property. In both situations the owner no longer has possession, but if property is lost the owner still wishes to retain ownership, whereas ownership is given up if property is abandoned. When property has been lost for a long period of time, it may be considered as no longer owned.

If someone simply loses an item of property at any time, ownership will be retained in the property. If a person loses a mobile phone in a shopping mall, the finder cannot acquire this by occupation. The owner of the phone will remain the owner. In such a situation the Civic Government (Scotland) Act 1982 Pt VI will apply. This statute governs both lost and abandoned property. It imposes on the finder of lost or abandoned property a duty to report the finding. If possession has been taken of the item, the duty extends to taking reasonable care of the item and handing it over. This must be to the police or a specified list of persons including the owner or the person entitled to possession. The police have a duty to take care of the property and attempt to find the owner. If the owner cannot be found after two months, the police have a discretion to give the property to the finder, sell it or otherwise dispose of it.

If property is abandoned or has been lost for a considerable period of time, it belongs to the Crown. This extends to treasure trove, which is property which has been buried or hidden at some point in time, presumably with the intention or hope of subsequent recovery. There are two interesting cases which illustrate both aspects of this rule on abandoned property.

In *Mackenzie v MacLean,* 1981 S.L.T. (Sh. Ct.) 40, a cargo of beer cans was partly damaged in transit by lorry from Fort William to Stornoway. On arrival at their hotel destination, the hotel owner was advised by the supplier to keep the undamaged cans and dispose of the rest. The bar manager and another employee were instructed to do this. A large quantity of cans had fallen on the road outside the hotel and others were placed in a skip. Many were taken by the locals, some of whom offered to pay for these. The two hotel employees accepted some money. They were charged with theft on the ground that the beer cans were technically abandoned property and belonged to the Crown. In the court case this position was confirmed although a not guilty verdict was returned as there was no *mens rea* for theft.

In *Lord Advocate v University of Aberdeen,* 1963 S.C. 533, which is known as the St Ninian's Isle Treasure Case, a team of students from Aberdeen University were on a field trip to St Ninian's Isle in Shetland and discovered eighth century treasure hidden underground. The University appropriated the treasure and took it to its museum in Aberdeen. The Lord Advocate on behalf of the Crown sued for delivery of the treasure. The University argued that the treasure was governed by udal law, which is a relict of the time when Shetland and Orkney belonged to Norway and part of which law still applies in Shetland and Orkney. Under udal law the finder of treasure would keep part of it. The Inner Division of the Court of Session held that Scots law applied, not udal law, and the Crown owned the treasure.

Abandoned property is sometimes referred to as *bona vacantia*. There are two further situations where property is, in effect, ownerless and belongs to the Crown. If a juristic person, such as a company, is dissolved and holds any property, such property will fall to the Crown as *bona vacantia*. When a person dies without a will and has no relatives however remote, the property of that person will fall to the Crown. In this case, the Crown is known as *ultimus haeres*, the last heir.

Accession

Accession is where two items of property become joined together in such a way that one item, the accessory, becomes part of the other item, the principal. If a new engine is fitted to a car, the engine will accede to the car. The engine, the accessory, becomes part of the car, the principal.

Accession can take place with different types of property. Moveable property can accede to heritable property which is a common form of accession. This is known as the law of fixtures and is discussed below. Heritable property can accede to other heritable property and moveable property can accede to other moveable property, as with the car and new engine.

Accession of moveable property to moveable property can occur naturally as when animals have offspring.[17] The owner of the animal will be the owner of the offspring. If a calf is born to a cow, the owner of the cow will automatically be the owner of the calf. This is one example of the principle of accession by fruits. Another example is that natural products of animals accede to the animal. A cow's milk is a natural product of a cow and the owner of the cow will own the milk it produces.

As noted below, accession can also take place with incorporeal moveable property, as when interest accumulates on a bank account. The owner of the bank account is entitled to the interest on the account.

Specification

Specification concerns property which is newly created from component materials and cannot revert back to its original components. When grapes are made into wine or corn into flour, it is not possible to turn the wine back into grapes or the flour back to corn. When such a new entity is created, the person who creates the new entity will become the owner of the new entity, even although the creator does not own the component materials.[18]

There are some requirements which must be satisfied before specification can take place. It is essential that a new entity comes into existence and the component parts cannot be separated back to their original state.[19] If they can, the component parts will belong to their original owners. If some pure gold is made into several plain gold rings, it is possible to melt the gold rings back into pure gold. Specification will not have taken place. If the gold is used along with other precious metals and jewels to create rings, specification will have taken place. It is also essential that the creator acted in good faith because the doctrine is an equitable one, although this has been doubted by some writers.[20]

In *McDonald v Provan (of Scotland Street) Ltd,* 1960 S.L.T. 231, a person acquired two cars. He cut them both in half and welded the front half of one to the back half of the other. He then sold this car to the purchaser. Some months later the police took away the car as the two cars had been stolen. In a subsequent court action, the seller argued that he had a right to sell the car as specification had taken place and he was the creator and owner of the car. The argument failed on the ground that the two halves of the car could easily be converted back into their component parts. It was also rejected on the ground that the creator was not in good faith.

When specification takes place, the owner or owners of the original component materials will be entitled to compensation for the cost of the materials. In *International Banking Corporation v Ferguson, Shaw & Sons,* 1910 S.C. 182, a company bought oil in good faith from another company who had no right to sell as it belonged to a different company. The purchasing company paid for and received the oil and manufactured lard which the company sold. The true owners succeeded in an action to recover the cost of the oil.

Commixtion and confusion

Commixtion and confusion occur when materials of the same kind which belong to more than one person are mixed together. These principles derive from the Roman law doctrines of *commixtio* and *confusio*. Commixtion applies to solids and confusion applies to liquids. If the mixing of the same items can be separated back, ownership will remain with the original owners. If a number of sheep belonging to different owners gather together in a field, there will be no change of ownership as the sheep should be capable of being identified by their respective owners, for example, by some form of marking. In contrast, if a quantity of flour or oil is mixed together, then commixtion or confusion will take place. In this case, the solid flour or liquid oil is owned in common by the owners of the constituents in shares corresponding to the amount and value of the contribution to the whole.[21]

If the mixing together of the solids or liquids produces something new which is different from its constituent parts, specification will take place, not commixtion or confusion.

Derivative acquisition or transfer

Derivative acquisition is the transfer of ownership to a new owner from an existing owner. Corporeal moveable property can be transferred in various situations such as gift, exchange, sale or loan. The rules on security for a loan are examined below. The rules relating to derivative acquisition are now no longer the same for all types of transfer. Originally the common law applied to all transfers, but in relation to sales, there is now extensive legislation under the Sale of Goods Acts and related statutes which governs this. This was introduced into Scots law under the Sale of Goods Act 1893 and the statutory rules differ considerably from the common law position.

Under the common law, there are two basic essentials for derivative acquisition to operate. These are intention and delivery. Erskine states:

> "Two things are ... required to the conveyance in this matter: First, the intention or consent of the former owner to transfer it upon some just or proper title of alienation, as sole gift, exchange, etc: Secondly, the actual delivery of it, in pursuance of that intention."[22]

As previously noted under the section on real rights and personal rights above, the first stage of intention, which is usually set out in an agreement in writing between the parties, only creates a personal right. The second stage of delivery is required to create a real right of ownership which is enforceable against the world.[23]

It is essential for the transfer to take place that the transferor has both title and capacity to transfer the property. In relation to capacity, this means that if the transferor is an individual, that person has contractual capacity to enter into the agreement and is not prevented from doing so by being under age or lacking in sufficient mental capacity. In relation to trustees or companies or other legal persons, this means that the trustees or company or other legal person are acting within their powers by entering into the agreement.

So far as title is concerned, it is a fundamental principle that it is not possible for someone other than the owner to transfer a good title to a property by mere delivery, without the owner consenting to or intending to transfer the property. This is known as *nemo dat quod non habet*, no-one can give what they do not have. Similarly, owners cannot transfer a more extensive right than their own.[24]

Delivery can be actual, constructive or symbolic. Actual delivery is obviously the most common situation. This is where the property is physically handed over to the acquirer or the agent of the acquirer or physical control is handed over, for instance, by means of a key.[25]

Constructive delivery occurs when a third party is holding property on behalf of the original owner and is instructed by the original owner to hold the property on behalf of the acquirer. It is essential before constructive delivery takes effect that the third party receives the instruction. If someone owns property which is in the possession of someone else and decides to give it to a friend, a letter instructing the person to continue to hold the property for the friend who is now the owner is constructive delivery. The letter of instruction must be received before this will be effective. In *Inglis v Robertson & Baxter* (1898) 25 R. (H.L.) 70, Goldsmith owned whisky in a bonded warehouse in Glasgow. The warehouse held this on behalf of him or his assignees and Goldsmith had a warrant to this effect. Goldsmith borrowed money from Inglis and endorsed and delivered the warrant to Inglis. This was not intimated to the warehouse keepers. In a dispute between Inglis and creditors of Goldsmith, it was held that as there had been no intimation to the third party holding the whisky, the real right to the whisky remained with Goldsmith.

Symbolic delivery occurs when the property or control of the property cannot be physically handed over and a symbol of this is handed over instead. The main example of this is a bill of lading, which is a document of title to goods which are in transit by ship.[26]

The rules for derivative acquisition under the Sale of Goods legislation are extensive and fairly complicated. They are beyond the scope of this book. The main governing statute is the Sale of Goods Act 1979. Goods are defined in the Act as items of corporeal moveable property excluding money. The basic rule for derivative acquisition or voluntary transfer is set out in s.17, which states that the property right of ownership in the goods will transfer when the parties intend it to be transferred. The parties are free to agree when this will be. It can be before or after the price is paid and before or after delivery of the goods. If ownership is not transferred when delivery is made, this is known as retention of title. There was some doubt as to whether this was valid under Scots law but this was confirmed in the case of *Armour v Thyssen Edelstahlwerke AG,* 1990 S.L.T. 891.

If the parties have not agreed on when ownership will pass, there are five default rules set out in s.18. The most important of these is the first one which states that where there is an unconditional contract for specific goods which are in a deliverable state, ownership passes when the contract is made. This flexibility is useful in commerce, but the parties have to be careful about the risks involved if the normal situation of ownership passing when the price is paid and the goods delivered is varied.

[15] Stair, II, i.33. Stair refers to the Roman law principle *quod nullius est, fit primi occupantis.*
[16] Wildlife and Countryside Act 1981; Protection of Badgers Act 1992.
[17] *Lamb v Grant* (1874) 11 S.L.R. 672.
[18] Stair, II, i.41.
[19] *North West Securites Ltd v Barrhead Coachworks Ltd,* 1976 S.C. 68, per Lord McDonald at 72.
[20] Bell, *Principles*, s.1298. Compare Carey Miller.
[21] Stair, II, i.37.
[22] Erskine, *Institute*. II, I, 18.
[23] Lord President Inglis in *Clark v West Calder Oil Co* (1882) 9 R. 1017 at 1024.
[24] *Scottish Widows Fund v Buist* (1876) 3 R. 1078 dealing with incorporeal moveable property.

[25] *West Lothian Oil Co Ltd v Mair* (1892) 20 R. 64.
[26] *Hayman v McLintock*, 1907 S.C. 936.

---

3. INCORPOREAL MOVEABLE PROPERTY

Incorporeal moveable property is property which is intangible and does not exist in a physical state. Such property can come into existence for the first time and be originally acquired. Most, but not all, rights to incorporeal moveable property can be transferred also. If a company issues shares or a person takes out an insurance policy, the new shares and the new policy benefits are new items of incorporeal moveable property. The shares can be sold to a new owner and the right to the proceeds of the insurance policy can be transferred to another person. A significant area of incorporeal moveable property relates to rights arising from original and creative works in cultural, scientific or business areas, known as intellectual property. This is an extensive area of law which continues to grow in importance and which has substantial specific legislation.

As with corporeal moveable property, the general rule is that there are two requirements for the transfer of incorporeal moveable property. Unlike corporeal moveable property, incorporeal moveable property is intangible and cannot be physically delivered to transfer ownership. The two requirements to transfer are assignation and intimation. Certain incorporeal moveable property cannot be transferred at all. Rights which are personal to a particular person, under the doctrine known as *delectus persona*, cannot be transferred, such as a contract of employment.

An assignation is the transfer of ownership from the assignor to the assignee. Technically, an assignation need not be in writing[27] but, in practice, it usually is. Some types of assignation, for instance, those relating to policies of assurance, need to have a certain form as laid down by statute.

Delivery of the assignation gives the assignee an effective personal right but the assignee will not obtain a real right against third parties unless there is intimation. There are various forms of intimation set out by statute[28] and various equivalents of intimation. If a debtor acknowledges the assignee's right, this may be equivalent to intimation. The transfer is effective from the date of intimation and if there are competing claims, the date of intimation will determine who has the right, not the date of assignation.

The effect of assignation is that the assignee takes the place of the assigner and succeeds to all the rights and obligations of the assigner. The assignee will have no greater right than the assigner and if there is a defect in the rights of the assigner, this defect will pass to the assignee.[29] In *Scottish Widow's Fund v Buist* (1876) 3 R. 1078, a Mr Moir took out an insurance policy and had stated that he was in good health in the proposal form. In fact, he was suffering from various diseases and was an alcoholic.

He assigned the policy to a Mr Buist. When he died the insurance company refused to pay out the proceeds due to the false statement and this was upheld by the court. Although Mr Buist was in good faith, the company would have been entitled to refuse to pay Mr Moir and Mr Buist had acquired no better right.

There is one exception to this rule. If there is a latent trust of which the assigner is unaware and the assignee takes in good faith and for value, the assignee will not be affected by the latent trust.[30]

Intellectual property rights

Intellectual property rights are incorporeal moveable rights which relate to original and creative works in cultural, scientific or business areas. They are creations of the human mind. This is a complex and expanding area of law. The main types of intellectual property are:

* patents;
* copyright;
* trade marks; and
* designs.

The following is a brief overview only of these property rights.

Patents

Patents are the oldest form of intellectual property rights. A patent gives the creator of an invention a monopoly right in respect of the manufacture and use of the invention for a period of 20 years. The main statutory provisions are in the Patents Acts 1977 and 2004. The invented product or process must satisfy several criteria. It must be novel, involve an inventive step, be capable of industrial application and must not be excluded from patentability. It requires some new characteristic which is not known in the body of knowledge in its field, referred to as prior art. It must show an inventive step which is not obvious to a person of average skill and knowledge in the relevant field. Subject matter which is not patentable includes scientific theories, artistic works and mathematical methods.

It is necessary to apply for a patent to the UK Intellectual Property Office which will normally grant a patent to the inventor if the requirements are satisfied. This will only give protection in the United Kingdom. It is possible to apply for patents in different countries. There is also a European Patent Office which will give protection in all the countries which have signed up to the 1973 European Patent Convention, as revised in 2000.

Copyright

Copyright can exist in a wide range of work. It covers three broad areas. These are:

* original literary, dramatic, musical or artistic work;
* sound recordings, films or broadcasts; and

• typographical arrangements of published work.

It covers visual, aural and written forms. It gives an exclusive right to make copies and reproduce the work of the creator. The main statutory provision is the Copyright, Designs and Patents Act 1988.

What is protected under copyright law is the expression of the original idea and not the idea itself. This extends to prohibiting unauthorised reproduction in all forms, including printing and sound recording, public performances and broadcasting, translation into other languages and adaptation, such as a novel into a screenplay for a film.

Unlike patents, there is no need to apply for copyright protection. Copyright protection exists provided that the requirements under the legislation are satisfied. The general rule is that the author is the first owner of copyright in a literary, dramatic, musical or artistic work. In this case, copyright lasts for 70 years from the death of the author. In films, the principal director and film producer are joint authors and the first owner of the copyright. Again copyright lasts for 70 years. For sound recordings, the period is 50 years from when the recording was first made and for broadcasts, it is 50 years from the first broadcast.

Copyright is protected against primary and secondary infringement and infringement is actionable unless there is a defence, such as use for certain educational purposes. Before using copyright material, the consent of the copyright owner must be obtained. There are several organisations, such as the Performing Rights Society, which acts on behalf of groups of copyright holders in connection with particular rights and can grant licences to users on payment of royalties. The rights protected by copyright are capable of being transferred, usually by assignation or granting of a licence.

Copyright is extended to include not only the foregoing copyright protections, but also the moral rights of the author or creator in certain copyright works. There are three main moral rights. The first is usually referred to as the paternity right and is the right to be identified as the author or creator. The second is usually referred to as the integrity right and is the right to object to any derogatory treatment of the work, such as adapting the work in such a way as to be prejudicial to the author or creator's reputation. The remaining moral right is the right not to have the work falsely attributed to someone else.

Trade marks
Trade marks are graphical signs which distinguish the goods or services of one undertaking from another. A sign can include words, numerals, logos, pictures or a combination of these. It can be the shape of goods or the way they are packaged. They enable the public to identify a particular business with the trade mark. A Coca Cola bottle has a distinctive shape which is protected by a trade mark, and even a scent may be the subject of a trade mark. They are protected under the common law principle of passing off and by registration under the Trade Marks Act 1994.

A trade mark can be registered with the UK Intellectual Property Office. Once registered, the owner of the trade mark is protected from use of

identical or similar marks for a period of 10 years, which can be renewed
for further periods of 10 years. The 1994 Act sets out various grounds of
refusal which are either absolute grounds or relative grounds. The former
are based on the nature of the trade mark itself. For instance, a mark will
not be registered if it does not have a distinctive character. The latter are
based on comparisons with similar existing trade marks.

Designs
Designs are similar to copyright and are the appearance of the whole or
part of a product resulting from lines, contours, colours, shapes, textures or
materials. Designs can be either functional or aesthetic. Certain designs
may be registered. Designs are protected automatically under the
Copyright, Designs and Patents Act 1988 if the requirements under this are
met. These are normally referred to as unregistered designs. The protection
extends to a period of 15 years after the creation of the design. Protection
is excluded where the design is necessary to make it fit with another article
to enable it to perform its function, or the design is necessary to match
another article with which it is associated.

Designs can be further protected by registration under the Registered
Designs Act 1949. The requirements are similar but not identical to the
requirements for protection under the 1988 Act. The design must be new
and have an individual, distinguishing appearance which is not determined
by its technical function. Registration gives an exclusive right to use the
design for five years and this can be renewed for further periods of five
years up to a maximum of 25 years.

---

[27] The Requirements of Writing (Scotland) Act 1995 s.11.
[28] Moveable Property (Scotland) Act 1862.
[29] *Scottish Widows' Fund v Buist* (1876) 3 R. 1078.
[30] *Redfearn v Somervail* (1830) 1 Dow 50.

---

4. RIGHTS IN SECURITY OVER MOVEABLE PROPERTY

Property can be used as security to obtain a loan or other benefit. This gives
the lender, the creditor, greater comfort in making the loan as there is better
protection if the debtor fails to pay. It may give the debtor the opportunity
to obtain a loan which might not be granted without the security.

When someone lends someone else money or incurs some other form
of debt, the creditor will have a personal right of action against the debtor
to recover the loan. This may be backed up by the existence of a personal
security granted by a third party as a guarantee of the loan, known as

caution. If the debtor fails to pay, the creditor has a personal right against the guarantor or cautioner. If a university law student requests a loan of £5,000 from a bank, it is highly unlikely that this will be given without any security. If the student's parents agree to act as guarantors, the loan may well be granted.

The creditor will be in a stronger position if he or she has not only a personal right, but also where there is some property which can be used as a real security which will give the creditor a real right against the world. Both heritable and moveable property can be used for this purpose. It is common place when a house is purchased for a bank or building society loan to be obtained to help finance the purchase and the house itself is used as a heritable security. This is discussed below. Moveable property can also be used for this purpose. If someone is short of cash, jewellery or other valuable moveable property can be taken to a pawn shop and handed over in exchange for a loan of money. In these cases, the property acts as security for the debt and gives the holder, the creditor, a preferential right over an unsecured creditor in the secured property. In the event of the granter of the security, the debtor, becoming insolvent, a secured creditor generally has a right to sell the secured property and be paid before the unsecured creditors.

A right in security is only an accessory right to secure the performance of an obligation, usually repayment of a loan. Once the obligation has been performed, the creditor must return the secured property to the debtor or grant an appropriate discharge. The right in security is redeemable and must be redeemed on performance of the obligation.

Rights in security can arise by agreement or by operation of law. Some rights are governed by common law and some by statute. There are different rules for the constitution of rights in security over different types of property. Generally, security rights over moveable property require delivery and it is not possible to obtain a security right over corporeal moveable property without possession of the property.[31] There are exceptions to this general rule.

Securities over corporeal moveable property

Securities over corporeal moveable property which require delivery can arise either by agreement, known as pledge or by operation of law, known as liens. Securities which do not require delivery are hypothecs and floating charges. Hypothecs have a fairly limited operation and floating charges are a special type of security which can be taken over both heritable and moveable property.

Pledge
A pledge is a simple contractual form of security. The owner of the corporeal moveable property, the pledger, makes an agreement with the lender, the pledgee, usually to borrow a sum of money. As part of the agreement, the pledger delivers the property to the pledgee as security for

the loan. The agreement need not be in writing but delivery is an essential element in pledge. The delivery may be actual, constructive or symbolic.

When the debt is repaid, the pledgee is bound to return the property to the pledger. If the debt is not repaid, the pledgee has the property in his or her possession as security. The pledge agreement will usually authorise the pledgee to sell the property to recover the debt. If it does not, the pledgee can apply to the court for authority to sell. The property which is pledged can only be used as security for the specific debt which is the subject of the pledge and not for separate debts which may be owed by the pledger to the pledgee.

Pawnbroking is a type of pledge although there are special rules for pawnbroking under the Consumer Credit Act 1974.[32] This is because pawnbroking is a business operated on the basis of pledges and protection for consumers is required. A pledge to a licensed pawnbroker must be in writing. When an item is pledged or pawned to a pawnbroker a receipt must be given. A pawn is generally redeemable for six months. Where it is not redeemed within six months or such other period which has been agreed, the pawnbroker has a statutory power under the Act to sell the property or to keep it if the debt is under £75.

Liens

A lien is a security right which arises by operation of law and results from the creditor being in possession of corporeal moveable property belonging to the debtor. A lien can be special or general. A special lien is the right of a creditor to retain a specific item of property until the debt incurred in relation to that property has been repaid. It arises in contracts for services based on the principles of mutuality of contract. This will often occur when something is handed over for repair. Until the repair bill is paid, the item can be retained exercising a special lien. If I take my watch to a jeweller for repair and when this is done I ask for my watch back and tell the jeweller to send me a bill, the jeweller can refuse to hand over the repaired watch until I pay for the repair.

A general lien is the right of a creditor to retain property of the debtor in possession of the lender until all the general debts due by the debtor have been settled, whether relating to that property or not. These liens relate to particular trades and several are usually recognised. A commercial agent or factor has a general lien over all goods, bills, money or documents of the principal which have come into the agent's possession during the employment of the agent.[33] This includes advances made to the principal, salary and commission and any liabilities incurred on behalf of the principal.[34] Such agents include stockbrokers. A banker has a general lien over all negotiable instruments belonging to customers which have come into possession of the bank in business transactions as opposed to mere deposit for safe keeping.[35] A solicitor has a general lien over all papers belonging to a client, including title deeds, wills and share certificates, for unpaid bills and expenses made in the ordinary course of business.[36] A hotelier or innkeeper has a lien over luggage of a guest for the amount of the hotel bill.[37] Certain items, such as clothes, are excluded.[38] This is categorised sometimes as a general and sometimes as a special lien.

As liens depend on possession of the property, they are lost if possession is lost. If the property subject to a lien can be sold, the creditor can apply to the court to sell the property if the debtor fails to pay the debt.

Hypothecs

Hypothecs give a creditor a right in security over corporeal moveable property without delivery to the creditor. The hypothec may be conventional or legal. A conventional hypothec arises by agreement. They are rare and are confined to maritime law.[39] They are curiously named as bonds of bottomry, relating to the ship itself, and bonds in *respondentia*, relating to the ship's cargo.

A legal hypothec arises by operation of law. There are certain maritime hypothecs which give a right in security over a ship, including a right to seamen in respect of unpaid wages and to the master in respect of properly incurred wages.[40] A solicitor has a hypothec over costs or property recovered in a court action for expenses incurred in the court action.[41] A landlord has a hypothec over certain corporeal moveable property in the leased premises belonging to the tenant as security for the rent. This used to apply to all types of leases including residential leases and small agricultural leases. It was abolished in relation to residential leases and agricultural leases under the Bankruptcy and Diligence etc. (Scotland) Act 2007 s.208(3) and is now restricted to commercial leases.

Floating charges

Floating charges were introduced in Scotland in 1961[42] and can be created over both heritable and moveable property. They are discussed below in the chapter on Securities over Heritable Property.

Securities over incorporeal moveable property

The rules for creation of a security over incorporeal moveables which cannot be delivered follow those for transfer of incorporeal moveables. They require assignation in security and intimation. In relation to company shares, a valid right in security requires a share transfer form and registration of this form with the company, subject to the right to transfer back to the debtor when the debt is repaid. Securities can also be granted over intellectual property, although no intimation is possible in respect of such property. There are certain specific rules regarding this, such as the requirement for an assignation of a patent to be registered in the Register of Patents.

---

[31] The Roman maxim *traditionibus non nudis pactis dominium rerum transferuntur* applies.

[32] 1974 Act ss.114–122.

[33] Bell, *Principles*, s.456.

[34] *Glendinning v Hope*, 1911 S.C. (H.L.) 73.

[35] Bell, *Principles*, s.1451.

[36] Bell, *Principles*, s.1438.
[37] Bell, *Principles*, s.1428.
[38] *Sunbolf v Alford* (1838) 2 M. & W. 248.
[39] Bell, *Principles*, s.456.
[40] Merchant Shipping Act 1995 ss.39–40.
[41] Solicitors (Scotland) Act 1980 s.62.
[42] Under the Companies (Floating Charges) (Scotland) Act 1961.

5. LANDOWNERSHIP

Historical background

The two key features of landownership in Scotland throughout the centuries have been the feudal system and registration in a public land register. The feudal system in Scotland dates back to the twelfth century and a public land register was first introduced in 1617.[43] Registration is discussed in the next section.

As noted in the introduction to this book, abolition of the feudal system was chosen as a symbolic, major reform by the first Scottish Executive following devolution in 1999 and was welcomed by the new Scottish Parliament without opposition. It triggered the series of Acts which have substantially modernised land law. Under the Abolition of Feudal Tenure etc. (Scotland) Act 2000, the feudal system was finally abolished on November 28, 2004. It is still important to know the basics of feudalism in order to properly understand the reasons for certain features of land law in Scotland.

Feudalism was introduced into Scotland as a social, political and economic system.[44] The fundamental principle of feudalism was that all land derives from the Crown as ultimate feudal superior. Originally, the King granted land to his nobles in the return for services to the King. These services were originally military service in the far off days of constant warfare. Land was not granted to the nobles outright, but was feued or transferred to them on a tenure, a type of holding of land, in return for the services, known as a *reddendo*. The nobles, in turn, were able to grant land to lesser mortals who actually worked on the land by subfeuing the land to them, again on a tenure in return for a *reddendo*, which might be agricultural services. The person who granted or feued the land was known as the superior and the person who received the land was known as the vassal.

The superior retained a right of ownership in the land as it was not granted outright and this right enabled the superior to claim and receive the *reddendo*. This right of ownership was known as *dominium directum*. The right of ownership of the vassal who received the land to use but without outright ownership was known as *dominium utile*. This meant that every time there was a grant of land and land was feued, or more correctly subfeued, there was a new link in a chain of ownership stretching back to the Crown as ultimate feudal superior. This ultimate ownership of the Crown was known as *dominium eminens*. From the Crown down to the person actually occupying and using the land, there was a feudal chain of ownership. A person would be, at the same time, the vassal of the superior who had subfeued to him and the superior of the vassal to whom he, in turn, had subfeued.

Originally, under the feudal system there were different types of tenure and *reddendo*, but by the twentieth century there was virtually only one type of tenure, feu farm, and one type of *reddendo,* feuduty or payment of money. Over the centuries substantial reform took place. The feudal system which was abolished in 2004 was very different from the original one and many of the features of feudalism had long since gone. In particular, since the mid-eighteenth century it was possible to transfer land not by subfeuing but by substitution without the consent of the superior.[45] This was where a vassal transferred land, not by subfeuing whereby the vassal became the superior of the vassal who was granted the land, but instead by stepping out of the feudal chain with the person granted the land becoming the new vassal of the original vassal's superior. Thus, instead of creating an additional new link in the feudal chain, the link was replaced by a substitute link.

Two further features of the feudal system are important. It was commonplace for a superior to insert feuing conditions, usually known as real burdens, in the title of the vassal when granting the land. These related to such matters as restrictions on the use that vassals could make of the land to protect the amenity of the neighbouring land. If such conditions were properly constituted, a superior would retain the right to enforce these conditions against the vassal. This could be done on the basis of simply being the superior even if the superior had no other connection with the land. To back up enforcement, it was usual to insert in the title of a vassal a right of irritancy which gave to a superior the ultimate power to take back the land if the vassal failed to observe the feuing conditions.

A major reform of the feudal system took place when the Land Tenure Reform (Scotland) Act 1974 abolished the right to create new feuduties. The Act also introduced provisions for most feuduties to be redeemed, or paid off automatically, when land was sold and for vassals to voluntarily redeem their feuduty. Both these cases involved the vassal making a one-off capital payment to the superior. Since 1974, the number of feuduties in existence rapidly diminished and it was estimated prior to the 2000 Act that less than ten per cent of land in Scotland was subject to payment of feuduty.

Under the Abolition of Feudal Tenure etc. (Scotland) Act 2000, the feudal system was abolished.[46] All superiorities were abolished and *dominium utile* became full *dominium* or outright ownership.[47] All feuduties were extinguished[48] and there were provisions for payment of compensation to superiors, which had to be claimed and were not paid automatically.[49] Other provisions in the Act deal with a former superior's rights to enforce feuing conditions and are examined in the section on Restrictions on landownership, below. Irritancies were also abolished.[50]

Registration

The key feature of landownership in Scotland, along with the feudal system, has been the need for registration in a public property register to complete a good title to land. Since 1617, a system of registration has existed in Scotland and the registration of a title to land has been necessary to complete a real right in the land. Most rights in land, whether they are outright ownership or a more restrictive property right, such as a right in security, require the title to such right to be in writing and the title deed to be registered. The Register of Sasines[51] was introduced in 1617[52] and was the basis of the system of land registration in Scotland for well over 300 years. Although the system was not perfect, it did work remarkably well. By the latter half of the twentieth century, however, it was felt that the system was becoming outmoded and a new system of land registration was introduced in 1979 with a new register, the Land Register. Eventually, all land in Scotland will be registered in the Land Register with the advantages this register brings.

The system of registration introduced in 1617 with the Register of Sasines is a system in which the register is a register of deeds only, not a register of title. The title to land does not flow from the register itself, but from the deed. The register acts as a public notice that the person has registered a particular title deed, but if that title deed is faulty, the register does not cure the defect. In contrast, the Land Register is a register of title where the title flows from the register itself and the Land Register does guarantee title. Once a title deed has been registered in the Land Register and the Keeper of the Register issues a land certificate, the land certificate is a guarantee that the holder has title to the land and this is backed up with a state guarantee so that the holder will be indemnified against any adverse action against the title.

It might seem that the Register of Sasines is a poor system of registration because a person cannot get a title which is free from challenge after registration, but the system is fortified by the operation of positive prescription. This is examined in the next section. The basic principle is that if a person has a title to land which is not obviously defective and possesses the land for the appropriate prescriptive period, the title becomes free from challenge. This system of registration in the Register of Sasines, plus the operation of positive prescription, lasted until the introduction of the Land Register in 1979. As it will be many years before the new system of land registration applies to all land in Scotland, it is the way certain land in Scotland is still held.

One other drawback of the system of registration in the Register of Sasines, apart from the lack of a guarantee of title, is inadequate description of the land in the register. There are various formal requirements for a title deed before it will be accepted in the Register of Sasines. These include the need for a description of the subjects. Many sasine title deeds do not contain plans of the subjects.[53] Those that do are often inaccurate. The subjects are described in words in the deed. These words are all too often vague or ambiguous. For instance, it may be impossible to tell where the physical boundaries lie. The operation of positive prescription may help, but all too often the position is unsatisfactory. The requirement for an accurate plan of the subjects would be a distinct improvement. This was one of the reasons for introducing a new system of land registration in 1979.

The Land Registration (Scotland) Act 1979 introduced a new system of land registration which will be gradually extended throughout Scotland. Land in Scotland was divided into operational areas and the provisions in the Act were introduced to these areas between 1979 and 2003. Land is only registered in the new Land Register on a sale and not, for instance, where it is gifted or subject to a security. It will be some time in the future before all land in Scotland is registered in the Land Register.

When land is first registered in the Land Register, the Keeper examines the title deeds to be satisfied that the person registering the title is the owner of the specified land. Once satisfied, the title is registered and a land certificate is issued which will have a plan attached. This will be an ordinance survey plan and will accurately delineate the boundaries of the land.

The certificate has four sections. These are:

- property;
- proprietorship;
- charges; and
- burdens.

The property section gives a brief description of the property which will often simply be the postal address and includes the ordinance survey plan. The proprietorship section identifies the owner and the date of registration of the title of the owner. The charges section details any securities over the property and their respective dates of registration. The burdens section details any burdens over the property. This will include any real burdens and servitudes and this is the only section in the land certificate which may be long. A land certificate is a more user friendly document than most deeds in the Register of Sasines. It is much easier to read and follow.

The effect of registration of title is that the title is guaranteed and indemnity will be paid if a subsequent problem arises with the title.[54] If the Keeper anticipates a potential problem because there is some doubt as to certain aspects of the title, it is open to the Keeper to exclude indemnity from part of the title.[55] For instance, there may be a doubt as to whether a piece of land forms part of the subjects actually owned by the person seeking to register. It may not be clear whether the person or the neighbouring person owns a strip of land which forms the boundary between them. In this situation, the Keeper may exclude the strip from indemnity. This means that ownership of the strip is not guaranteed, although an unchallengeable right may be acquired by prescription.

A fundamental principle of the new land registration system is that it should be possible to know the exact position relating to the title by looking at the entry in the Land Register. This is subject to a qualification in relation to what are known as overriding interests. There are certain burdens or encumbrances which will automatically affect the title even if they do not appear in the Register.[56] The most important of these are servitudes and unregistered leases for less than 20 years. Some servitudes are registered but others are not. Provided the servitude is validly created, it will be a right over the registered land even though it does not appear in the burdens section. Similarly, a tenant under a valid lease has the right to occupy the subjects of the lease although the lease is not referred to in the Register. These matters are discussed further in the appropriate sections on Servitudes and Leases below.

A key essential of the land registration system is that the Register should be accurate and can be relied on to be so. It follows from this that it should not be possible to change the Register once a title has been registered and a land certificate issued, as this would undermine its reliability. The reality is that mistakes can inevitably occur as no system is perfect. The 1979 Act recognises this and it is possible for the Keeper to alter the Land Register in certain circumstances. This is known as rectification. It is only possible in limited circumstances but this is becoming a problem area in the current land registration system.

Under the 1979 Act s.9, the Keeper can rectify an inaccuracy, but cannot do so if the rectification would prejudice the proprietor in possession except in four situations. This is linked to the provisions on indemnity in s.12 which provide that a person is entitled to indemnity if they suffer a loss as a result of the Keeper rectifying the Register or refusing to rectify the Register. The four situations are:

- to note an overriding interest;
- where all affected persons consent;
- where the inaccuracy was wholly or substantially caused by the fraud or carelessness of the proprietor in possession; and
- where indemnity is excluded.

On the face of it, these seem reasonable exceptions, but this places great emphasis on being the proprietor in possession. In *Kaur v Singh,* 1999 S.C. 180, there was some indication that the parties who were in dispute as to who was entitled to the property had gained entry to the property and changed the locks on more than one occasion, in an attempt to be the proprietor in possession and have the benefit this brings. In *Safeway Stores Ltd v Tesco Stores Ltd,* 2004 S.C. 29, rival supermarkets, Tesco and Safeway, placed and moved marker poles in a river bed in attempts to establish possession. The problem is that the Act does not define what exactly is meant by the proprietor in possession and this is not entirely clear.

There is a further problem relating to the rectification and the accuracy of the Register following a series of cases involving the trustee of a Mr Short, which circumvented the rule protecting the proprietor in possession.

Mr Short sold flats to Mr Chung at less than full value. Mr Chung in turn transferred these as a gift to his wife. Mr Short became insolvent, was then sequestrated and a trustee appointed. Under insolvency law, if property belonging to a sequestrated person has been transferred without the full price being received within a certain period prior to the sequestration, this is regarded as a gratuitous alienation and the transaction is challengeable by the trustee. This was the case here and Mr Short's trustee took action to recover the property.

First he obtained a reduction of the deeds transferring the title to Mrs Chung.[57] He was able to do this as the transfer to Mr Chung was voidable as a gratuitous alienation and the transfer to Mrs Chung was also voidable as she was not a purchaser in good faith for value. He then endeavoured to have the decree of reduction registered in the Land Register. The Keeper refused to register on the ground that this was not possible and the title on the Register could only be altered by rectification. The trustee disputed this but in the second court case which went all the way to the House of Lords the court upheld the Keeper's position.[58]

It might have been expected that the trustee would then seek a rectification of the Register which would have been refused as Mrs Chung was the proprietor in possession, and this would result in payment of indemnity to the trustee due to a loss caused by refusal to rectify. Instead, the tenacious trustee was determined to recover the property and took a different tack. He asked Mrs Chung to transfer the properties to him and when she refused he raised a third case to compel her to do so. He was successful in this case and at last recovered the properties.[59] Mrs Chung was not able to get any indemnity as there had been no rectification.

The problems surrounding rectification and indemnity and other difficulties relating to the current land registration system under the 1979 Act have led to a comprehensive review of the system by the Scottish Law Commission and reform of the system is likely to take place some time in the future.[60]

A further problem with registration generally arose following the case of *Sharp v Thomson,* 1997 S.C. (H.L.) 66, although subsequent developments diminished the potential problems the case posed. Prior to that case, it was accepted that registration in the appropriate register was essential to create a real right and that any earlier stage, such as the delivery of the title deed by a seller to a purchaser, would not create a right greater than a personal right. This case threw considerable doubt on this fundamental principle.

In *Sharp v Thomson*, the Thomsons purchased a flat from a company, Albyn Construction Ltd. The contract stage, the missives, was concluded. The company had a floating charge over its whole property including the house sold to the Thomsons. Due to a departure from normal conveyancing practice the document transferring the title to the Thomsons, the disposition, was delivered late and then not registered straight away. Before the disposition was registered, the company went into receivership and the floating charge "crystallised" over the assets. The question was who received the house? Scottish land law was clear that the receivership should take precedence over the Thomsons as the disposition was not recorded and that was the decision of the Inner House of the Court of Session. The House of Lords reversed this. It is not entirely clear what the grounds for this were and it is tempting to conclude that the real reason was that any other result was manifestly unjust. The reason is now generally taken to be an interpretation of the actual words used in company legislation relating to receiverships. Nevertheless, the decision did seem to go against a fundamental principle of Scottish land law and was subject to much criticism.

Subsequent to *Sharp v Thomson,* it was hoped that this deviation from the principle that registration is essential to create a real right would only apply to situations involving a receivership. This was confirmed in the case of *Burnett's Trustees v Grainger,* 2004 S.C. (H.L.) 19, where there was a failed attempt to extend this deviation to the sequestration of an individual. In this case, a house was purchased, missives concluded and the disposition delivered but not registered by the purchaser. The seller was then sequestrated and the trustee in sequestration of the seller registered his title before the disposition was belatedly registered by the purchaser. The Sheriff Principal held that the House of Lords' decision in *Sharp v Thomson* also applied to a sequestration. His decision was overturned by the Inner House of the Court of Session who ruled that the decision in *Sharp v Thomson* did not apply to a trustee in sequestration situation. This was upheld by the House of Lords.

Prescription

Prescription is an important principle in Scottish property law. Prescription may be negative or positive. The function of negative prescription is to extinguish rights which have not been exercised. The function of positive prescription is to create rights in land or render existing rights unchallengeable. Both types of prescription have existed under the common law and there was a statute on prescription as early as 1617.[61] The main statute dealing with the modern law of prescription is the Prescription and Limitation (Scotland) Act 1973. The most important changes over the years have been to the length of the various prescriptive periods.

The way negative prescription operates is quite simple. If someone has a property right but has not exercised this right for whatever reason for the appropriate period of time, the right is lost. The two main periods of negative prescription set out in the 1973 Act are known as the short negative prescription and the long negative prescription. The short negative prescription period is five years[62] and the Act sets out various rights, such as the right to receive payment of rent under a lease, which will be extinguished if not exercised during the period.[63] The long negative prescription period is 20 years[64] and affects such rights as a servitude right of way which will be similarly extinguished if not exercised during the period.

Positive prescription operates to create a right or to fortify an existing right. Under the Land Register system, there is no need for prescription.

Since title is guaranteed, someone with a land certificate knows that his or her title cannot be challenged. It is not the same under the Register of Sasines system as it does not guarantee title. It is possible for two people to have a title deed registered which includes the same piece of land. The Register of Sasines is only a register of deeds not a register of title. In this situation, prescription can assist one of the two to obtain an unchallengeable title. This requires the registered title which includes the piece of land, plus actual possession of the piece of land for the necessary period. Both may have a registered title but both cannot have possession.

The system of registration of a deed in the Register of Sasines depends on the operation of positive prescription to ensure that the registration system functions effectively. For positive prescription to operate, a person must have a suitable title to an interest in land which is registered and have had suitable possession of that interest for the appropriate prescriptive period. Both title and possession are required for positive prescription. If someone satisfies both these requirements, that person acquires a good, unchallengeable title to the land in question. The 1973 Act sets out the nature of the title and possession which is required.[65] Positive prescription usually applies to the right of ownership of land but also applies to other rights such as servitudes,[66] recorded leases[67] and salmon fishings.[68]

The title must be *ex facie* valid and not forged under s.1(2) of the 1973 Act. *Ex facie* valid means that the title appears valid on the face of the deed and there is no obvious defect, such as the deed being unsigned. The deed must be sufficient to include the relevant piece of land. For example, if the description of the property has clear boundaries, it will not be possible to acquire ownership of anything beyond these boundaries by prescription, even if there is possession of land beyond the boundary.

There is no requirement of good faith on the part of someone registering the title. It used to be possible to record what is known as an *a non domino* disposition which means the person recording the deed is not the owner. If such a deed was registered relating to a piece of land and the person registering subsequently had the requisite possession of the land for requisite period, that person would acquire a good, unchallengeable title to the land. This practice is no longer possible as the Keeper of the Registers of Scotland will not accept an *a non domino* disposition and it has been held that such deeds do not have the necessary title required for prescription to operate in the recent case of *Board of Management of Aberdeen College v Youngson*, 2005 S.C. 335.

The possession must be for the appropriate period and openly, peaceably and without judicial interruption under s.1(1) of the 1973 Act. Openly simply means that the right has been possessed in an obvious and unsecretive way. Peaceably simply means that there has been no dispute over the possession. Without judicial interruption means that the possession has not been challenged by some court or similar action.[69]

The appropriate period is 10 years for most interests including the right of ownership,[70] 20 years for rights in respect of the foreshore and salmon fishings[71] and also in respect of recorded leases[72] and positive servitudes and public rights of way.[73]

Positive prescription is one area of property law which has been subjected to scrutiny in the human rights context and in a recent case, *J A Pye (Oxford) Ltd v UK* (2006) E.H.R.R. 3, the question of whether prescription violates human rights by depriving a person of their property was considered. The European Court of Human Rights eventually ruled that it did not.

Extent of landownership

If a person owns heritable property or land, various questions arise as to the extent of that landownership. What exactly is the physical extent of the landownership? What are the actual property rights that go with ownership of the land? To what extent is an owner of land restricted in the use and enjoyment of the land? The first two questions are now dealt with under the sections on Physical extent of landownership and Incidents of landownership and the third under the following section on Restrictions on landownership.

Physical extent of landownership
The physical boundaries of land with neighbouring land will be determined by the title deeds. In an ideal world, all titles to land will have an accurate plan attached which clearly sets out where the physical boundaries are. This is one of the aims of the Land Register introduced in 1979 whereby all title deeds of all land in Scotland will have an ordinance survey plan showing the physical boundaries. This will not happen for some considerable time until all land in Scotland is registered in the Land Register. Meantime, many title deeds registered in the Register of Sasines do not have accurate plans or have no plans at all. The question of where the boundaries are must be determined by a construction of the wording in the title deeds. All too often the wording is vague or ambiguous in such titles and boundary disputes are not uncommon.

Where the description in the title deeds is referred to as a "bounding" description, this will normally contain specific details of the boundaries and will be sufficient to accurately identify the actual boundaries. Where there is an ambiguity, prescription may establish the extent of the land and where the boundaries are. If a landowner has a recorded title that on the face of it could be interpreted as including the boundary which the landowner claims is the true boundary, and the landowner possesses the land contained by that boundary peaceably, openly and without judicial interruption for the prescriptive period of 10 years, that boundary will normally become the legal boundary. The position is not straightforward, however, and this whole area is a problem one for conveyancers.

Landownership is theoretically from the heavens to the centre of the earth. The Latin maxim for this is *a coelo usque ad centrum*. This means that a landowner owns the airspace above the land and the ground strata below. This allows a landowner to prevent encroachment into the airspace by such things as overhanging branches of a neighbour's tree or a tower crane. In *Halkerston v Wedderburn* (1781) Mor. 10495, Mr Wedderburn's garden in Inverness had elm trees in it. The branches of the elm trees grew to overhang his neighbour, Mr Halkerston's property. Mr Halkerston was annoyed and went to court. The court decided that Mr Wedderburn was bound to prune his trees so that they would not overhang Mr Halkerston's property. Although not actually decided in the case itself, this case is usually taken as authority for a neighbour's right to remove an encroachment of branches of trees.

This right to prevent enchroachment into airspace is subject to limitations. A landowner cannot prevent aeroplanes flying overhead. There is statutory provision to allow aeroplanes to fly over property at a reasonable height under the Civil Aviation Act 1982. Further upwards, there is legislation dealing with space exploration and outer space. Below the ground there are also restrictions. Certain precious metals belong to the Crown under a statute dating back to 1424, the Royal Mines Act 1424. This Act has the distinction of being the oldest property statute in Scotland which is still in force. Similarly, petroleum and natural gas also belong to the Crown under the Petroleum Act 1998. Coal and the right to mine for coal vests in the Coal Authority under the Coal Industry Act 1994. Other minerals are included with landownership but the right of ownership to these can be severed.

In a tenement, as discussed below, in the absence of provisions in the title deeds, ownership extends vertically to the mid-point of the joist separating upper and lower individual flats. Ownership of the air space above the roof belongs to the ground floor flat owner.

One final point to note in relation to the actual boundaries of landownership is that, in rare cases, these may change under the principle of accession. This can happen gradually over a period of time where, for instance, a river forms the boundary between properties. The course of the river may slowly and imperceptibly change, and over a long period land from one property may be deposited on another property. The principle involved is known as alluvion. When this happens, the land so deposited accedes to the land on which it is deposited. Alluvion does not take place where there are seasonal fluctuations. This is known as avulsion and has no effect on ownership.

Fixtures

Ownership of land includes ownership of any buildings on the land under the principle of accession. When moveable items are attached to a building or to land, these items may become part of the building or land by accession and be converted into heritable property. The law on this is known as the law of fixtures and it is an important area of law, particularly when properties are sold or transferred, or when someone who has had possession of land as a tenant gives up possession. It is a practical concern whether an item of moveable property has become attached to the building or land as a fixture and has become part of that building or land. The moveable item might belong to one person and when it becomes a fixture belongs to another person.

In some situations it is obvious that something which is moveable has become a fixture by accession. If I build a porch on to the front door of my house, the building materials are moveable before the porch is constructed but once the porch has been built it attaches to the house and accession takes place. If I paper the walls of my house, the wallpaper is moveable but attaches to the house itself once pasted. Conversely, if I place a large compost bin beside my garden shed or hang some pictures on my walls, it is clear that these are temporary attachments and accession has not taken place. In other situations, it may not be entirely clear whether an item of moveable property has become a fixture.

The law on this has developed over a long period of time and various criteria are generally recognized as essential for an item to become a fixture by accession. These are:

- physical attachment;
- functional subordination; and
- a degree of permanency.

There must be some degree of physical attachment. The greater the physical attachment, the more likely it is that accession has taken place. The contrasting state of wallpaper and pictures is very apparent, but in between these extremes are situations which are far from clear. In *Cochrane v Stevenson* (1891) 18 R. 1208, paintings on a panel which were attached to a wall by metal plates and which exposed a bare wall on removal were held not to be a fixture.

Items may not have any actual physical connection other than sitting on land and still be regarded as a fixture. This will happen if the weight of the item is very substantial, as in *Christie v Smith's Ex.,* 1949 S.C. 572, which involved a summerhouse weighing two tons.

Functional subordination means that the use of the moveable item is subordinated to the use of the heritable property. The item is attached for the improvement or better enjoyment of the property. If kitchen units are installed in a kitchen in a house, it is obvious that the function of these is to provide storage cupboards and worktops which will enhance the kitchen. They will become fixtures. In *Assessor of Fife v Hodgson*, 1966 S.C. 30, storage heaters installed in a house were held to be fixtures.

There must be some degree of permanency before a moveable item becomes a fixture. This will vary according to circumstances but the attachment must be more than temporary. In *Brand's Trustees v Brand's Trustees* (1876) 3 R. (H.L.) 16, mining machinery was installed in premises leased by a tenant for use in the tenant's business. The tenant died and the question was who owned the mining machinery? Prior to this case, it was generally understood that the position in Scots law was that if moveables were introduced on to land and were removeable, they did not become a fixture and that the intention of the parties was a relevant factor. The machinery in dispute was removeable and the tenant intended to remove this at the end of the lease. The case was decided by the House of Lords with three English judges sitting. These judges assumed that the law on fixtures was the same in Scotland and England and applied English law in their decision. English law was different. It provided that mining machinery was a trade fixture which belonged to the landlord on the tenant's death, unless previously removed. Accordingly, they decided that the machinery belonged to the landlord. The intention of the parties was held to be irrelevant.

This House of Lords case has been criticised as imposing English law on Scots law, but it does illustrate that what is permanent is a matter of degree. If there has been some alteration made to the principal property which enables the moveable item to be physically attached, this will strengthen the argument in favour of the moveable item becoming a fixture. In *Scottish Discount Co v Blin*, 1986 S.L.T. 1023, permanent foundations were installed in premises used for a scrap business and very substantial shears were placed on these. In addition, shelters were built to protect the shears. This factor was taken into account by the court which ruled that the shears were fixtures, even although they had been dismantled and removed by the time of the court case.

A further factor which will tend to indicate a sufficient degree of permanence is whether the item can be removed without damaging the heritable property. If it can, it may be more likely to be regarded as moveable and vice versa, but this is only an indicator. Similarly, if the installation and removal of the item involves considerable time and expense, then this also increases the chance of the item being regarded as a fixture.

It would seem logical that the intention of the parties should be a relevant factor, whereas the case of *Brand's Trustees* ruled that it is not. Subsequent cases appear to allow some room for consideration of the apparent intention of the parties making the attachment, determined from the type of item and the heritable property and the nature of the attachment.

Even though the item has become a fixture by accession, there may be a right to remove the fixture in certain circumstances. This right to remove applies to certain trade fixtures which the tenant has introduced for business purposes, illustrated in *Syme v Harvey* (1861) 24 D. 202, which involved glass houses in a nursery garden, and certain agricultural fixtures in agricultural holdings under the Agricultural Holdings (Scotland) Act 1991 s.18. It is not clear whether tenants can remove certain domestic or ornamental fixtures, as is the case in England.[74]

Crown rights

Various rights of property vest in the Crown as sovereign. These Crown rights are known as *regalia*. *Regalia* are divided into two types, *regalia majora* and *regalia minora*. The former are held by the Crown in trust for the public and cannot be sold. This means that such rights are, in practice, public rights. The latter originally belonged to the Crown but could be disposed of by the Crown by sale or other means and are now under the control of the Crown Estate Commissioners.

In addition to the Crown *regalia,* the Crown has absolute ownership of the sea and the seabed up to the territorial limit of twelve miles. This used to be regarded as part of the *regalia majora* but it is now accepted that the Crown can sell or lease parts of the seabed. For example, leases of the seabed for fish farming are not uncommon. The Crown also owns the bed, the *alveus,* of tidal rivers.

The *regalia majora* are the right to navigate, moor temporarily and fish for white fish in relation to the sea, the foreshore and tidal navigable rivers. The foreshore is that part of a beach which lies between the high and low water marks of the spring tides. In addition, the public have a right of access for recreation to the foreshore under the common law.

The *regalia minora* are the right to certain precious metals under the Royal Mines Act 1424, treasure and lost property, salmon fishings and the foreshore itself. Salmon fishings are a separate property interest in land, confusingly referred to as a separate tenement. As with all *regalia minora,* such an interest in land may have been sold by the Crown at some point and this right to fish for salmon can be a very valuable property right. The owner of salmon fishing rights has the ancillary right to access the river and fish from the river bank. Similarly, part of the foreshore may have been sold by the Crown in which case the owner of the foreshore is subject to the public rights mentioned above.

Law of the tenement

Tenements are a very prevalent type of property in Scotland. The word usually conjures up the vision of a large stone building of several storeys in which there are a number of flats. Such buildings are very common in urban Scotland, but a tenement under Scottish property law need not be a large building and covers a very extensive range of properties. Until recently, the law governing tenements, which is generally referred to as the law of the tenement, was the common law which was developed over the years and was based on principles of individual property, common property and common interest. As this common law of the tenement proved to be increasingly problematic in certain areas, particularly in relation to repairs, a new statutory law was introduced in the Tenements (Scotland) Act 2004, following recommendations by the Scottish Law Commission.

A tenement under s.26(1) of the 2004 Act is defined as a building or part of a building which comprises two or more flats which are separately owned and divided horizontally. Thus a tenement includes properties which vary from a traditional or modern multi-storey block of flats to a house which has been converted into an upper and lower flat. As a result, many properties in Scotland are governed by the law of the tenement. The law applies regardless of whether the flats are used for residential or other purposes.

It is important to note that the title deeds of many flats in tenements include specific provisions which deal with the matters covered in the 2004 Act, including ownership and liability for repairs. If this is the case, these provisions will apply to the respective flats in the tenement and not those in the Act. This is because the law under the Act, as was the common law prior to the Act, is only a default law which will apply only in the absence of specific provisions in the title of individual properties.

It follows that if the title of a property covers a particular matter on which there is a default position in the Act, the title will apply. If there is no such provision, the default law will apply. It may be the case that the title specifically deals with some matters covered by the Act but not all. In this case, the default law will apply to those matters on which the title is silent. This means that there can be a combination of specific provisions in the title plus the statutory default law. This might not be ideal and care is required in making specific provision which changes the default law. This was also the position under the common law and a relatively recent case illustrates the difficulties which can result if the drafting of the provisions in the title are either defective or incomplete.

In *Rafique v Amin*, 1997 S.L.T. 1385, there was provision in the title deeds of certain flats in a tenement which purported to alter the common law of the tenement in respect of common property and the provisions were not properly worded to achieve the position which was intended. It was held in the case that one proprietor had an absolute right of veto to prevent alterations to the common property which was patently not what was intended. Lord Justice-Clerk Ross stated:

> "It is somewhat ironical that if, instead of making these elaborate provisions regarding common property, the grantor had allowed the more usual law of the tenement to prevail, many of these difficulties [in this case] would not have arisen".

The 2004 Act deals with ownership of the various parts of a tenement. It largely restates the existing common law but clarifies areas of doubt or difficulty which existed. It introduces a statutory form of common interest to replace the common law, again largely restating the existing common law position. The Act introduces a default scheme of rules relating to liability for repairs to the tenement and decisions regarding repairs known as the Tenement Management Scheme. This is a significant innovation which tackles one of the problem areas which existed under the common law. The Act also covers a variety of miscellaneous matters such as access rights, nuisance and demolition to give a new, comprehensive law of the tenement.

Ownership

Ownership of the various parts in a tenement is established under the 2004 Act in two ways. Section 2 of the Act gives the extent of what is owned by individual flats and the boundaries between them is set out by referring to sectors. In s.3, the remaining parts of the tenement, referred to as pertinents, are allocated using a service test. These two sections clearly cover who owns what under the Act and will apply in the absence of provisions in the title. These can now be examined in some detail.

Sectors under s.2 include the individual flats, closes or common passage and stairs, lifts and any other three dimensional space such as a cellar. If there is a boundary between two contiguous sectors, that boundary will be the mid-point. This means that a wall separating one flat from an adjacent flat or the close is owned to the mid-point. Similarly, joists or floors/ceilings separating a flat from the flat below or above are also owned to the mid-point. If a boundary is not shared with another sector, for example, internal walls in a flat and the section of the external wall enclosing that flat, the boundary is owned solely by that flat. Where a door or window serves one flat exclusively, such as a door to an individual flat from the close, there is an exception to the general rule and the door or window is owned solely by that flat owner.

Special provision is made for the top and ground floor flats. The top floor flat includes the roof over that flat and the ground floor flat includes the *solum* under that flat. A close includes the roof over and the *solum* under the close. These provisions follow the common law. It means that where there is more than one top floor or ground floor flat, the owner of the respective flats will own the section of the roof or *solum* which is above or below the flat.

So far as the roof is concerned, the position under the common law was a little complicated. It was clear that the top flat owner owned the roof space above the flat and under the actual roof, but the air space above the roof presented problems. Following the general principle that land is owned from the heavens to the centre of the earth, it was the ground floor flat which owned the air space above the roof. This meant that if the owner of the top floor flat constructed a dormer window in the roof, this technically would encroach into the air space of the ground floor flat and could be objected to, unless the owner of the ground floor flat acquiesced. The Act confirms the ownership of the air space above the roof goes with the ground floor flat, but sensibly makes specific provision under s.2(7) to deal with the problem of dormer windows. This subsection provides that where the roof slopes, the sector which includes the roof extends to the level of the highest point of the roof. This encompasses the triangular air space in which a dormer roof can be constructed.

Most parts of the tenement are covered under these provisions in s.2. The remaining parts are dealt with in s.3. These are the close, the garden and various miscellaneous parts. Ownership of these pertinents is determined by who needs to use them and is either common property or individual property.

Ownership of the close or common passage and stair was not clear under the common law. The close is usually used by all flat owners in a tenement but to a different extent. All use the ground floor entrance and passage when there is no separate entrance for a ground floor flat, but only the top floor flat owners need to regularly use the whole stairs to the top floor. The close was clearly common property but it was not authoritatively established whether the whole close was owned in common by all or only by those who used the various parts of the close. The Act makes the position quite clear. The close is the common property of all flat owners who use it for access and this extends to any lift, except a lift which serves one flat only. A main door flat which provides access to one flat only is owned by that flat solely and is excluded from common ownership.

The garden ground is owned by the ground floor flat or flats to the extent which it is adjacent to that flat. This excludes paths, outside stairs or other means of common access.

For the remaining pertinents, such as fire escapes, rhones, pipes and cables, ownership is determined using a service test. If the pertinent serves only one flat, it is owned solely by that flat. If it serves more than one flat, it is owned in common by the flats which it serves. There is a helpful provision which states that the whole of such a pertinent, for example, an entry phone system, is owned in common and not just the part actually used. This is analogous to the position relating to the close.

Finally, there is a special provision that chimney stacks are owned in common by the flats served by the stack in proportions calculated by reference to the number of flues in the stack.

Common interest

The principle of common interest is the means whereby flat owners in tenements are protected from any activities by one of them in relation to his or her flat which adversely affects the fabric of the tenement to the detriment of the others. This was well established under the common law and is re-enacted under the 2004 Act ss.7–10. An owner of any part of a tenement which provides support or shelter to another part must maintain that part and this duty can be enforced by any affected owner. This duty is strengthened by a prohibition on any action which would or is likely to impair such shelter and support. The duty does not apply if it would not be reasonable, having regard to all the circumstances including the age and condition of the building and cost. This means that the duty would not apply if the tenement was badly dilapidated or derelict. There is provision for recovery of costs from the other flat owners as part of the general rules on repair and liability for costs which were introduced in the Act under the new Tenement Management Scheme.

Repairs

One of the main problem areas with tenements under the common law was the position relating to repairs, especially to common property. There were difficulties in obtaining agreement on the need for repairs and in recovering the cost of repairs from those liable to pay. Much of this stemmed from the general rule that where property is owned in common, all owners have to agree to matters of management in relation to that property. It was also unfair that top floor flat owners, for instance, were saddled with the cost of repairs to the roof which could be very expensive and affected everyone in the tenement. As a result of these difficulties, many tenements in Scotland were in a poor state of repair. The 2004 Act tackled this problem by introducing the Tenement Management Scheme which will apply in the absence of specific provisions in the title. The key feature of this innovation is that the liability for repairs to parts of a tenement building is separated from the ownership of these parts.

The Act provides details of the scheme in s.4 and Sch.1. Certain property within the tenement is categorised as scheme property and there are detailed provisions in relation to this. Scheme property is extensive and covers external, gable and load bearing walls, the *solum* and foundations, the roof and all parts of the tenement which are common property. Decisions regarding the management of scheme property, including repairs but not improvements, can be taken by a majority of the flat owners with each flat owner having one vote. This is a significant and welcome change to the common law need for consent by all. A scheme division can include the important provision that owners are required to make a deposit of their estimated share of the work in advance.

Once a scheme decision has been taken, all flat owners must be notified. There is a 28 day period before any work, other than emergency work, can be started to allow an opposing owner or new owner to challenge the decision in the Sheriff Court. The Sheriff has power to overturn the decision if it is not in the best interests of all the owners or unfairly prejudicial to one or more owner.

The Tenement Management Scheme also sets out the liability for scheme costs. The basic rule is that each flat owner is liable for an equal share of the cost. This is subject to several exceptions. If the cost relates to common property, the liability is in accordance with the individual share which will usually be equal. If the flats vary significantly in size and the floor area of the largest flat is more than one and a half times that of the smallest flat, the liability is apportioned in accordance with floor area. There is a special rule regarding the section of the roof over the close which allocates liability equally, unless the size of the flats triggers the exception already noted, in which case it will be apportioned accordingly.

In the case of emergency repairs, one flat owner can instruct or carry out these and this will be regarded as if it was a scheme decision, allowing the flat owner to recover appropriately any costs personally incurred.

As already noted, there are further provisions in the Act dealing with various miscellaneous matters, including the position when ownership of a flat is transferred with repairs outstanding or unpaid, insurance and access rights.

Incidents of landownership

Landownership includes the right to exclusive possession of the land and to use and enjoy the land. Exclusive possession includes the right to prevent trespass and encroachment. The right to use and enjoy the land includes the right of support, certain rights in water, certain game and fishing rights and the right to be free from nuisance. These rights are sometimes collectively known as incidents of landownership and are now examined in turn.

Exclusive possession
A landowner has the right of exclusive possession of the land and the basic principle resulting from this is that the landowner can exclude others from the land. This possession is referred to as natural possession where the landowner physically occupies the land personally. It is open to the

landowner to give the right of actual physical possession to someone else, for example a tenant under a lease. Where this happens, the possession by the tenant is known as civil possession on behalf of the landlord landowner.

This right of exclusive possession is only the starting point. There has been increasing statutory intervention allowing various people to enter on land which the landowner is powerless to prevent, culminating in the extensive rights of access to land granted under the Land Reform (Scotland) Act 2004. When the Bill which led to the Act was going through the Scottish Parliament, it was the subject of considerable controversy and this has continued since the Act was passed.

One category of persons granted rights to enter on land is relatively uncontroversial. These are officials under various Acts who are given this in the public interest. For instance, gas board officials under the Gas Act 1995 and health and safety inspectors under the Health and Safety at Work etc. Act 1974 are granted this right. Similarly, in an emergency a person can enter land and will not do so unlawfully if escaping from a fire or a similar hazard on adjacent land. Bell also mentions the pursuit of a criminal as a justifiable intrusion.

Subject to these qualifications and those under the 2004 Act, it follows from the right of exclusive possession which a landowner enjoys that landowners should be free from trespass or encroachment on their land.

Trespass and encroachment

Trespass is where a landowner's right of exclusive possession is encroached by the temporary intrusion of someone on the land. Trespass is not by itself recognised as a crime in Scotland, although there are certain statutes which deal with specific situations, such as the Night Poaching Act 1828. The reality is that there is very little a landowner can do against a single act of trespass. The landowner can ask the trespasser to leave but cannot use force unless the trespasser threatens violence to person or property.[75] Trespass by itself is not a civil wrong either, but if damage is caused, the trespasser may be sued. It may be possible to obtain an interdict against trespass but this is unlikely be granted if the trespass is trivial or if repetition of the trespass is not expected.[76] An interdict was refused in relation to a straying pet lamb in *Winans v Macrae* (1885) 12 R. 1051.

A landowner can endeavour to prevent trespass by notices, alarms or barbed wire, although this must be qualified in relation to the new legislation on public access to land, discussed below. Also, there are practical limits on what can be done and landowners have a duty of care to trespassers under the Occupiers' Liability (Scotland) Act 1960. This effectively prevents the use of such things as booby-traps. A guard dog is permitted but there are rules on control and warnings in the Guard Dogs Act 1975.

Encroachment is where a landowner's right of exclusive possession of the land, including the airspace above the land, is interfered with. Encroachment into airspace has already been noted. Encroachment can also take place on or below ground. If roots from a neighbour's tree grow into land this is an encroachment on that land. If the owner of minerals under a landowner's land extracts these without permission or express title to do so, this will also be an encroachment. As with trespass, the usual remedy against encroachment is interdict.

Public access rights to land

Under the Land Reform (Scotland) Act 2003 Pt 1, new rights of public access to land have been introduced which are often referred to as "the right to roam". This Act is one of the series of Acts introduced to modernise Scottish land law following devolution. As part of this modernisation, the Scottish Parliament wished to improve public access rights to the countryside and other land. The details of this are controversial, but there are now extensive rights of public access to land in addition to existing rights. Section 1 of the Act confers statutory access rights on land to everyone. These allow the public to be on the land for specified purposes or to cross the land. These purposes must be recreational, educational or commercial, provided it is one which could also be non-commercial, such as acting as a mountain guide.

Certain land is excluded from these rights.[77] This includes buildings, school grounds, sports fields, building sites and land on which crops have been sown or are growing. Also excluded is sufficient land adjacent to houses to allow a reasonable measure of privacy to ensure that enjoyment is not unreasonably disturbed. This is not precisely defined and has resulted in several high profile cases. A further exclusion is where the land has been open to the public on payment of a fee. This is intended to exclude existing tourist attractions, such as Blair Drummond Safari Park.

These rights of access must be exercised responsibly by those using them[78] and landowners must manage their land responsibly to take account of these rights of the public.[79] Landowners are specifically prohibited from taking action to prevent exercise of these rights such as putting up notices, obstructions or leaving animals at large.[80] Enforcement powers are given to local authorities.[81]

A Scottish Outdoor Access Code has been drawn up by Scottish Natural Heritage, as provided for in the 2003 Act and approved by the Scottish Parliament. This sets out in detail how rights of access should be exercised responsibly.

It might be expected that the provisions which exclude access for reasons of privacy would be a potential area of dispute and this has proved to be so. At the time of writing there have been three reported cases on the legislation decided by the courts and two of these relate to this issue.

The first one, *Gloag v Perth and Kinross Council,* 2007 S.C.L.R. 530, attracted a considerable amount of publicity as it involved a well-known business woman, Ann Gloag and one her homes at Kinfauns Castle, near Perth. Kinfauns Castle is set in around 23 acres of ground. Mrs Gloag wanted to maintain her privacy and erected a six foot barbed wire fence around part of the castle comprising the castle itself, the immediate garden and an area of woodland totalling around 11 acres. She sought declarator under s.28(1)(a) of the 2003 Act that the land within the barbed wire fence was not land in respect of which access rights were exercisable. The application was opposed by Perth and Kinross Council and the Ramblers Association. The sheriff decided in favour of Mrs Gloag. There was no appeal.

The Sheriff's decision was subject to considerable criticism and critics went so far as to suggest that the decision undermined the clear intention of the Scottish Parliament. As there is little guidance on the matter in the Act itself, cases will be decided on their individual merits. In a subsequent case, *Snowie v Stirling Council,* 2008 S.L.T. (Sh. Ct.) 61, a much smaller area of ground was declared exempt from public access rights. The property involved was Boquhar House, Kippen and the owners had sought to have the whole estate of 70 acres declared exempt.

The third case on public access rights reported so far is *Tuley v Highland Council,* 2009 S.L.T. 616, which is an Inner House case dealing with the management of public rights of access by a landowner who was keen to encourage responsible access.

Right of support

Land will collapse if it is not supported. Support is necessary from below and also from surrounding land to prevent collapse or subsidence. It is a natural right of a landowner to receive such support and any operations beneath the land or on neighbouring land which cause surface damage can lead to a claim for damages. It is not necessary to prove negligence. Such a right of support arises automatically by law. In other situations a right of support may be implied in all the circumstances. An automatic right of support only arises in respect of the land itself and not buildings on the land, but such a right may be implied. This question usually arises when minerals are excavated under the land. In *Angus v National Coal Board,* 1955 S.C. 175, the case concerned an action of damages brought after an agricultural worker died due to subsidence in a field where he was working and under which a colliery company had formerly worked coal.

Lord Justice-Clerk Thomson stated,

> "The right of support is an incident of property ... owner, in virtue of his ownership, has the right to have his land left in its natural state and he enjoys that right *qua* owner. If the owner's right of support is breached, he becomes entitled to damages for surface damage without requiring to establish negligence."

The right to work minerals may be reserved by a previous owner. In such cases a right of support of buildings will be implied where the buildings were already on the land at the time of reservation, where there was an obligation imposed in the title to erect buildings when the reservation was made or where the erection of buildings was clearly foreseen at the time of reservation.[82]

If buildings are damaged as a result of operations by a neighbouring landowner this may constitute a nuisance.[83]

Various statutes make provision for loss of support or damage. In the case of coal and the right to mine coal which is vested in the Coal Authority, when this is exercised there are provisions relating to compensation and remedial works relating to this in the Coal Mining Subsidence Act 1991.

Water rights

The law on water rights is established under the common law, although there are various statutory provisions which may affect the position, such as those on control of pollution. In particular, the Water Environment and Water Services (Scotland) Act 2003 implements a recent European Water Law Directive and introduces a new licensing scheme for the extraction of water.

The Crown has extensive rights in water, particularly in the sea, sea lochs and tidal rivers as part of the Crown *regalia*. Landowners may also have water in some form as part of the land they own, which requires consideration. Water can be running water, such as rivers and streams, or still water such as a loch or a bog. Running water is ownerless.[84] Still water which lies on the surface of land or water which percolates through the ground belongs to the owner of the land. This can be extracted by a well and can be used for manufacturing purposes even if it would otherwise flow to a stream.[85] Such water can be discharged onto a lower landowner's land if it naturally flows that way, but not in a polluted state.[86]

Lochs are either sea lochs or fresh water lochs. A sea loch is equated to the sea and belongs to the Crown. As regards other lochs, if the loch is completely surrounded by a landowner's own property, the landowner has full rights of ownership in the loch. Where a loch is surrounded by land belonging to different landowners, the bed of the loch, known as the *alveus*, is owned by each landowner adjacent to his or her land up to the centre of the loch. The loch itself, with the right to sail on it and catch fish in it, other than salmon, is owned in common.

The rights relating to rivers and streams depend on whether they are navigable or non-navigable. If a navigable river is tidal, the Crown owns the *alveus* but the public have a right to navigate and to fish in the river, except for salmon, and to moor boats temporarily on the river.[87]

If the navigable river is non-tidal, the banks and the *alveus* to the midpoint of the river are owned by the riparian owners, those owning land up to the banks of the river. This is subject to the public's common law right of navigation. There is also a common interest in the flow of the water and a riparian proprietor cannot do anything to interfere with the quality of the water or the amount of flow.[88]

The question of whether a river is navigable and the extent of the right of navigation can be a matter of dispute. In *Wills' Trustees v Cairngorm Canoeing & Sailing School Ltd*, 1976 S.C. (H.L.) 30, it was held that a one-way right of navigation existed where logs had been floated down a river to the sea from time immemorial.

If the riparian owners interfere with the public right of navigation, this can be challenged. In *Orr Ewing & Co. v Colquhoun's Trustees* (1873) 4 R. (H.L.) 116, the owner of land on both banks of a river constructed a bridge across the river. Two of the piers were built in the water. From time immemorial, small vessels had used the river to get from the River Clyde to Loch Lomond. Objection was taken to this artificial structure in the river. The Inner House of the Court of Session held that the river was a public navigable river and no one had a right to erect structures on the bed of the river. The House of Lords reversed this decision and held that, while the public may have a right of navigation in a non-tidal navigable river, the proprietors of the *alveus* are entitled to erect structures on it, unless the structure so erected would actually interfere with and obstruct navigation.

If a river is non-navigable, the position is similar, except there are no public rights. The riparian proprietors own the banks and the *alveus* to the mid-point of the river. These riparian owners have a common interest in the water and they can use their section of it for sailing and other activities, subject to the same restrictions which prevent interference with the quality or flow of water. Each owner can take water from the river for drinking or washing even if this diminishes the flow, but not for any commercial purpose, unless there is no change to the flow or quality of the water.

Fishing and game rights

The right of ownership includes the right to fish in lochs, rivers and streams belonging to the landowner. Tidal navigable rivers and lochs belong to the Crown and the public has a right to fish in these, other than for salmon. If there is more than one owner of a river, each riparian owner has the right to fish to the mid-point of the river. The riparian owners must fish from their own side, but it is possible to cast their rods across the mid-point. The right to fish does not include salmon unless this is separately owned, as salmon fishing forms part of the *regalia minora* of the Crown. Salmon fishing is regulated by statute, principally under the Salmon and Freshwater Fisheries (Scotland) Act 2003.

Certain animals are classed as game under various statutes and these include hares, rabbits, pheasants and grouse. A landowner has the right to kill game on the land. It is possible and common to lease shooting rights. The right belongs to the owner, not the occupier and a tenant does not have the right unless specifically leased to the tenant. There are also various statutory provisions aimed at preventing poaching, including the Night Poaching Act 1828 and the Poaching Prevention Act 1862.

Freedom from nuisance

A landowner is entitled to be free from actions and behaviour by other landowners which interferes with the enjoyment of the land. Such conduct may constitute a nuisance under the common law and is considered in the next chapter on Restrictions on landownership.

---

[43] Registration Act 1617.
[44] See generally Reid, *The Law of Property in Scotland* (Butterworths, 1996), paras 41–113 (written by Professor G. Gretton); Gordon, *Scottish Land Law,* 3rd edn (W.Green, 2009), Ch.2.
[45] Tenures Abolition Act 1746.
[46] 2000 Act s.1.

[47] 2000 Act s.2.
[48] 2000 Act s.7.
[49] 2000 Act s.8.
[50] 2000 Act s.53.
[51] Sasine means the act of giving and taking possession of land.
[52] The Registration Act 1617.
[53] No record of plans attached to deeds was kept at Register House prior to 1924 and plans were only automatically recorded from 1933.
[54] 1979 Act s.12.
[55] 1979 Act s.12 (2).
[56] 1979 Act s.28.
[57] *Short's Tr v Chung*, 1991 S.L.T. 472.
[58] *Short's Tr v The Keeper of the Register of Scotland*, 1996 S.C. (H.L.) 14.
[69] *Short's Tr v Chung (No.2)*, 1999 S.C. 471.
[60] SLC Discussion Papers No. 125 (2004), No.128 (2005) & No.130 (2005).
[61] Prescription Act 1617.
[62] 1973 Act s.6.
[63] 1973 Act Sch.1.
[64] 1973 Act s.7.
[65] 1973 Act s.1.
[66] 1973 Act s.3.
[67] 1973 Act s.2.
[68] 1973 Act s.1(2).
[69] The appropriate actions are set out in s.4.
[70] 1973 Act s.1(i)(a).
[71] 1973 Act s.1(4).
[72] 1973 Act s.2.
[73] 1973 Act s.3.
[74] *Spyer v Phillipson* (1931) 2 Ch. 183.
[75] *Wood v North British Railway Co* (1899) 2 F. 1.
[76] *Hay's Trustees v Young* (1877) 4 R. 398.
[77] 2003 Act s.6.
[78] 2003 Act s.2.
[79] 2003 Act s.3.
[80] 2003 Act s.14.
[81] 2003 Act Ch.5.
[82] *Caledonian Railway Co v Sprot* (1856) 2 Macq. 449; *North British Railway Co v Turners Ltd* (1904) 6 F. 900.
[83] *Lord Advocate v The Reo Stakis Organisation Ltd*, 1982 S.L.T. 140.
[84] Stair states "running waters are common to all men, because they have no bounds; but water standing, and capable of bounds, is appropriated", II.i.5.
[85] *Milton v Glen-Moray Glenlivet Distillery Co* (1898) 1 F. 135.
[86] *Montgomerie v Buchanan's Trustees* (1853) 15 D. 853.
[87] *Crown Estates Commissioners v Fairlie Yacht Slip Ltd*, 1979 S.C. 156.
[88] *Young & Co v Bankier Distillery Co.* (1893) 20 R. (H.L.) 76

6. RESTRICTIONS ON LANDOWNERSHIP

Although theoretically an owner of land is unrestricted in the use and enjoyment of the land, there are various restrictions on this use. These restrictions are imposed for the benefit of other landowners and for the public generally. They may exist to limit the activities of a landowner which may be detrimental to neighbours or to the public. They may exist to give another landowner certain rights over the land. They may also exist to regulate land which is owned or used in common. As noted in discussing Bell's classic definition of ownership above, these restrictions may be imposed by the law itself or may be agreed by the owner. When agreed by the owner, they are usually inserted in the owner's title as title conditions and are either real burdens or servitudes.

Real burdens and servitudes are interrelated but have different origins, as servitudes derive from Roman law and real burdens were developed in the nineteenth century as a practical necessity when property was sold. The law under the common law was complex and uncertain in parts, particularly in relation to real burdens. There were various areas of difficulty, such as entitlement to enforce real burdens and the ability to extinguish a real burden. There were some, but insufficient, statutory provisions. As part of the comprehensive review of land law undertaken after devolution, this complex area of law was reviewed by the Scottish Law Commission and this led to the Title Conditions (Scotland) Act 2003, which came into force on November 28, 2004. This simplifies and modernises the law on real burdens and servitudes to a large extent, although some problems remain. It is fair to comment that the law on real burdens created after the Act came into force is clear and coherent, but the position relating to real burdens created before then is not free from difficulty. Real burdens and servitudes need to be examined in some detail below.

It can be noted that the 2003 Act deliberately uses the term "title conditions" and details the type of conditions covered by the Act. This encompasses both real burdens and servitudes and includes others such as conditions in long leases.

Restrictions at common law and by statute

Various restrictions are imposed by law on the use and enjoyment of land. This is both under the common law and extensively by statute. The restrictions under the common law are sometimes referred to as the law of neighbourhood, as the underlying principle is that a landowner cannot use land in such a way as to interfere with a neighbour's use and enjoyment of the neighbouring land. Under the common law, such interference may amount to a nuisance which is a delictual wrong.

Nuisance
A nuisance can be caused to the public generally as well as to neighbours. Nuisance is defined by Bell as:

> "Whatever obstructs the public means of commerce and intercourse
> ... Whatever is noxious or unsafe, or renders life uncomfortable to
> the public generally, or to the neighbourhood; whatever is

intolerably offensive to individuals, in their dwelling houses, or inconsistent with the comfort of life..."[89]

Various factors are taken into account to ascertain whether or not a nuisance has been committed, including the nature of the harm suffered and the nature of the conduct causing the harm. There are not many recent cases on nuisance, due to the fact that there are many statutory provisions which deal with conduct which may also be a common law nuisance.

A relatively recent case was brought on the basis of nuisance and is worth noting. In *Webster v Lord Advocate,* 1984 S.L.T. 13, the owner of a flat adjacent to and overlooking Edinburgh Castle esplanade sought an interdict against nuisance by noise caused by the erection of scaffolding for the Edinburgh Military Tattoo and the Tattoo itself. It was held that the Tattoo itself was not a nuisance but the noise from the erection of steel scaffolding was, although the interdict was postponed for six months to allow the Tattoo to proceed and to allow a system of scaffolding erection to be considered which did not involve a nuisance.

The usual remedy against a nuisance is an interdict. If damage has been caused it will be necessary to establish *culpa* or blame before damages can be recovered.[90]

Spite
Another common law restriction which is rarely but occasionally established is where the conduct of a landowner is regarded as spiteful and is for no other purpose than to cause harm to neighbours. The Latin maxim for this is *aemulatio vicini.* Older cases deal with such matters as erecting a wall on a boundary to block out a neighbour's light,[91] but more recently, shutting off a water pipe which supplied the pursuer and ran through the defender's garden was held to be within the doctrine in *More v Boyle*, 1967 S.L.T. (Sh. Ct) 38.

Statutes
As discussed below, real burdens developed in the nineteenth century as there were only a limited number of statutes which imposed any controls on the development and use of land. This is no longer the case and in the modern highly regulated society we live in, there are now many statutes which impose a wide range of restrictions on how land is used. These include legislation on town and country planning, building control, the countryside, public health, housing and civic government, health and safety at work and environmental matters. In all these statutes in these areas and many more there is some restriction on the use a landowner can make of land.

Real burdens

A real burden is defined in the Title Conditions (Scotland) Act 2003 as:

"An encumbrance on land constituted in favour of the owner of other land in that person's capacity as owner of that other land."[92]

It is an obligation in respect of the land which is inserted in the title to that land for the benefit of another landowner. If it is properly constituted, it will be enforceable against the owner of the burdened land for the time being by the owner of the other land for the time being and is said to "run with the land". Often these burdens have been inserted long ago, but they remain enforceable against the burdened proprietor by the benefited proprietor.

Feudal and non-feudal real burdens
Under the feudal system, it was usual for the superior to insert real burdens in the title of the vassal to restrict the use of the land by the vassal. This originally served a useful purpose in the days before there were any statutes dealing with such matters as planning restrictions, development control and pollution. These burdens acted as a social control on land which would otherwise be uncontrolled. If a superior retained other land in the vicinity, it was in the superior's interest that land in the community was properly regulated.

Originally, feudal burdens did not cause problems and they existed for good reason. Over a period of time, the way they operated became unfair in many situations. Where superiors retained property in the community, it was quite understandable that they should have the right to enforce these burdens, but if the burden was created as a feudal real burden, this right to enforce continued even when they had disposed of all the property in the neighbourhood. Just by being the superior entitled the superior to enforce feudal real burdens. If there was a feudal real burden relating to a property in Dundee, for example, and the superior lived in the south of England, the superior could still enforce the burden if the vassal in Dundee was about to contravene the burden. This led to a situation where the only reason a superior would seek to enforce a burden was for financial gain. Until the introduction of the Lands Tribunal in 1970, it was virtually impossible to change or get rid of a feudal real burden without the superior's consent. Superiors were prepared to consent to this, but only on payment of a fee. Thus the original laudable reason for introducing real burdens was being misused by superiors and was one of the reasons for the recent final abolition of the feudal system.

Real burdens could also be created in transfers of land which were not feudal transfers by subinfeudation but by substitution. Such burdens are non-feudal burdens and were created in ordinary dispositions as opposed to feu dispositions. These burdens continue in force after the abolition of the feudal system.

Under the abolition of the feudal system implemented by the Abolition of Feudal Tenure etc. (Scotland) Act 2000, superiors were abolished along with all feudal trappings. The person who was previously the superior could no longer enforce a feudal real burden simply by being the superior. Feudal real burdens could no longer exist as a feudal real burden. It was recognised in the legislation that certain feudal real burdens should be allowed to continue as they still served a legitimate purpose. A period of time was provided in which superiors were able to convert feudal real burdens into non-feudal real burdens provided that they satisfied the requirement for these. Thus some feudal real burdens were duly converted and remain as normal real burdens today.

Types of Real Burden
Real burdens can be affirmative or negative. An affirmative real burden is a positive obligation, such as to erect a fence and maintain this in all time coming. A negative real burden is a restriction on use, such as to refrain from using a house for anything other than residential purposes. An affirmative or negative burden may have an additional burden related to its purpose known as an ancillary burden.

Most burdens are praedial, which means that both a benefited and burdened land is required. The burden must be for the benefit of the land itself or a community of land and not simply for the owner of the land. Such a benefit would be a personal benefit and not a real benefit. The whole concept of a real burden is that it is for the benefit of whoever happens to be the owner of that land for the time being, which will change from time to time. The 2003 Act, however, introduced a new type of non-praedial burden, known as a personal real burden, which appears a contradiction in terms.

There are eight specific types of personal real burden, the most important being a conservation burden. In this new type of burden there is a burdened land but not a benefited land. The right to enforce the burden against the owner of the burdened land is given to a specific legal person, as opposed to a benefited land. In conservation burdens under s.38 of the 2003 Act, the benefited person can be one of a number of conservation bodies, for example, Scottish Natural Heritage, and the purpose of the burden in the burdened land is to preserve or protect the architectural, historical or other special characteristics of the land for the benefit of the public. In this case, Scottish National Heritage and Scottish Natural Heritage only can enforce the burden against whoever owns the land in question.

Apart from these new personal real burdens, all real burdens are praedial. One type of real burden which existed prior to the 2003 Act is formally referred to as a community burden under s.25 of the Act. This is where a burden is imposed on a common scheme of two or more units and each unit is both the benefited and burdened property. In other words, the burden is created and inserted in all the titles of a community for their mutual benefit and is mutually enforceable.

A simple example of a community is a housing scheme. If there is a cul-de-sac of seven houses, it is obvious that what each of the owners does in his or her home may affect the six neighbours. If one owner dumps rubbish in his or her garden and allows it to become untidy and overgrown, this will be unsightly and the other six owners will be affected. They will see the unkempt garden, weeds will spread to their gardens and their amenity will be adversely affected. A community burden to keep the garden in a neat and tidy condition can be enforced by them all against the neglectful owner. If this neglectful owner turns over a new leaf and the next door neighbour then neglects the neighbouring garden, the now reformed owner can enforce the same burden against that neighbour, along with the other owners.

Community burdens are one of two main types of real burdens. The other is a neighbour burden, although this term is not used in the Act. Most burdens which are not community burdens are neighbour burdens. A neighbour burden is where a burden is created in the title of a neighbour for the benefit of the person who is selling the land. In these burdens there is only the burdened and benefited land and the burden is only enforceable one way, unlike community burdens. A typical example would be if someone sells part of his or her garden for the erection of a house and imposes various real burdens in the title of the piece of ground sold off to preserve amenity.

The 2003 Act makes specific mention in s.35 of facility and service burdens which are a type of community burden. The former are where the facility regulates the maintenance, management or reinstatement of the use of services, for example, a private road. The latter, which are rare, relate to the supply of services to other land, for example, a water supply.

Creation of Real Burdens
One of the criticisms of real burdens under the common law was a lack of transparency. The existence of a burden was not as clearly defined as it might be and it was frequently not entirely clear who had the right to enforce the burden. The 2003 Act reformed both the creation and enforcement of real burdens with this criticism in mind.

It is important to be familiar with the rules on the creation of real burdens both before and after the Act came into force on November 28, 2004, as a burden which was validly created before the Act will continue to be a valid burden. The new rules for creation of real burdens only apply to burdens created after the Act came into force.

The way the Act tackles the creation of new burdens is to largely re-enact the existing rules for their creation under the common law and add three new requirements to improve these rules, particularly with the need for greater clarity in mind. The re-enactment of the common law rules and the new requirements are examined in turn.

The common law rules for creation are set out in the leading case of *Tailors of Aberdeen v Coutts* (1870) 1 Rob. App. 296. The dispute in this case involved a disposition by the Tailors of Aberdeen to George Nicol of part of Bon Accord Square in Aberdeen. Mr Nicol undertook a number of obligations including, in particular, an obligation to build houses and to pay two thirds of the cost of forming and enclosing the central square. Mr Nicol then became insolvent and the subjects were sold and conveyed to Mr Coutts. The essential question was whether the obligations imposed on Mr Nicol in the disposition were enforceable against Mr Coutts. The Court's judgment sets out in detail the requirements for the constitution of real burdens. These are:

- clear intention to burden the land not the person;
- the burden is for an exceptional purpose;
- the burden is expressed in clear terms; and
- the burden is registered in the Register of Sasines.

These rules are more or less re-enacted under the new rules for creation in ss.3–6 of the 2003 Act. These can now be more accurately stated as:

- the burden must be praedial for the benefit of the land, excepting community burdens which must be for the benefit of the community and personal real burdens which must be for the benefit of a specified person;
- the burden cannot be illegal;
- the burden cannot be contrary to public policy, such as an unreasonable restraint on trade;
- the burden cannot be repugnant with ownership;
- the burden cannot impose a monopoly; and
- the burden must be set out in a constitutive deed and be registered.

Various other cases under the common law have clarified aspects of these rules. It is to be expected that a burden must be for an acceptable purpose and not be illegal, contrary to public policy, impose a monopoly or be repugnant with ownership. An example of the last aspect would be an attempt to prevent a landowner having the right to lease the land. An unsuccessful attempt to create a monopoly was discussed in *Aberdeen Varieties v James F Donald (Aberdeen Cinemas) Ltd,* 1939 S.C. 488.

It is also not unexpected that a real burden must be in clear and unambiguous terms. There is a presumption that landownership is free from restriction and any restriction is strictly construed *contra proferentem,* that is against the person wishing to apply the restriction. Examples of wording rejected as too vague and ambiguous by the courts include a restriction against any building "of an unseemly description" in *Murray's Trustees v St Margaret's Convent Trustees,* 1907 S.C. (H.L.) 8, and a prohibition against any operations the superior "may deem objectionable" in *Meriton Ltd v Winning,* 1995 S.L.T. 76, although the court did consider that the wording may be appropriate in certain circumstances. In *Anderson v Dickie,* 1915 S.C. (H.L.) 74, a purported real burden was inserted in a title deed to impose conditions on part of the ground attached to a mansion house. The wording referred to "the ground occupied as the lawn". This was held to be too imprecise wording for the constitution of a real burden.

Under the Act, it is provided that the real burden must be set out in a constitutive deed which will usually be in the individual title deeds themselves but may be in a separate deed of conditions.

The three new requirements for real burdens created after the Act are:

- the burden must be called a real burden or a specific type of burden, such as a community burden;
- the burden must identify both the burdened and the benefited land; and
- the burden must be registered in the title of both the burdened and benefited land.

These three provisions greatly improve the transparency of real burdens. The first requirement is not particularly significant but makes it quite clear that a particular provision in a title is a real burden. The second requirement to identify both the burdened and benefited land is very significant because under the common law it is often unclear who has the right to enforce a real burden. Who is subject to the burden is not a problem but who has the right to enforce it often is a problem, as discussed in the following section. The third new requirement of dual registration is a major improvement. Under the common law rules, the existence of a burden is clear from the burdened title as that is where the burden is set out. Conversely, the burden is not set out in the benefited title and it is not clear from the title of the benefited proprietor that the burden actually exists. This will not be the position now with all newly created burdens. The existence of the real burden will be obvious from the title of both the burdened and benefited land.

Enforcement of Real Burdens

A validly created real burden exists as a restriction on the burdened land and can be enforced against the owner of the burdened land by the owner of the benefited land. Enforcement is not automatic and the owner of the burdened land must satisfy certain requirements before the burden can be enforced. The only persons who did have an automatic right to enforce were superiors in respect of feudal real burdens unless they had lost the right. Feudal real burdens no longer exist. So far as non feudal burdens under the common law are concerned, the right to enforce these was problematic and was a key issue addressed by the 2003 Act. Basically, the problem is due to the fact that it is possible to have an implied right to enforce as well as an express right under the common law.

It is not possible to have an implied right to enforce new real burdens under the 2003 Act. As discussed above, one of the new requirements for the creating of a valid real burden is the need to specify the benefited land or community, if it is a community burden. This means that the person who has the right to enforce is expressed in the real burden. The problem of implied rights of enforcement in real burdens created prior to the Act remains a problem area despite the provisions in the Act, as we shall see shortly.

Under the common law, it is necessary to have both a title and an interest to enforce a real burden. This is repeated in the 2003 Act which provides in s.8(1) that a real burden is enforceable by any person who has both a title and interest to enforce it. Prior to the abolition of the feudal system, only superiors had these automatically.

Under the common law, only the owner of the benefited property was in a position to satisfy these requirements to enforce. This was extended in the Act under s.8(2) to include a tenant of the owner of the benefited property and the non-entitled spouse of the owner. These are important extensions as it may well be a tenant or non-entitled spouse who will be affected by any contravention of the burden and who will wish to enforce it.

As regards title, there is no problem with real burdens created after the Act because they require the benefited property to be named and the burden must be registered in the title of both the burdened and benefited property. The title to enforce is clearly expressed. It is also possible to have an express title to enforce under the common law and this presents no difficulty. The person who originally inserted the real burden in the title and the successors to the title of that person will have this. The difficulty lies in the possible existence of an implied title to enforce under the common law.

This implied right to enforce is known as a *jus quesitum tertio* which, if established, gave a neighbouring proprietor the right to enforce a real burden without an express title to do so. This is in addition to the proprietor with an express right to enforce. The law on this was developed in the leading case of *Hislop v MacRitchie's Trustees* (1881) 8 R. (H.L.) 95 and was complex and not entirely clear. In simple terms, if the title creating the real burden was one of a number of titles granted to neighbouring landowners by the same person and all of these titles had the same real burdens, known as a common scheme, and there was clear reference to this common scheme or a mutuality of community interest amongst the landowners, then each landowner was able to enforce the real burdens against each other. This law was subsequently developed in further cases, notably *JA Mactaggart & Co v Harrower* (1906) 8 F. 1101, but the position remained uncertain and imprecise. It created practical difficulties for a burdened proprietor who might not know who exactly was able to enforce the burden in the title. Implied rights could extend to a number of proprietors which potentially could be quite large and all these proprietors might be able to enforce.

Implied rights to enforce real burdens are abolished under s.49 of the Act, but the common law rules on implied rights are replaced with new statutory implied rights in respect of existing real burdens under ss.52–54. The rules established in *Hislop* are abolished but are largely re-enacted. Unfortunately, difficulties under the common law are set to continue.

Section 52 sets out a provision which is very similar to the rule in *Hislop*. If real burdens are imposed under a common scheme and the deed by which they are imposed expressly refers to the common scheme or is worded to imply a common scheme, the proprietors of these properties in the common scheme will have mutually enforceable implied rights, provided there is nothing in the deed to contradict this, such as the grantor reserving a right to vary the burdens.

Section 53 extends the provisions in s.52 by giving implied enforcement rights to what are referred to as "related properties", although there is no definition of what this term means. Section 54 gives implied rights in the special situation of sheltered and retirement housing.

In relation to facilities and service burdens, it is implied that any property which benefits from the facility or service will be a benefited property under s.56 of the Act.

These statutory implied rights, especially those in s.53, have been subject to considerable criticism and continue the uncertainty in this part of the law on real burdens. Further analysis of this is beyond the scope of this book.

As regards interest, under the common law there is a need to have a patrimonial interest to enforce the burden except for superiors whose interest is implied. A patrimonial interest means that the property of the person concerned is affected by the burden and would suffer detriment if it is not enforced. It is possible to have an interest at some point which is subsequently lost due to a change in circumstances. Section 8(3)(a) of the Act provides the statutory requirement which is now necessary for an interest to enforce. It states that such an interest exists if failure to comply would result in material detriment to the value or enjoyment of ownership. This may seem straightforward but a controversial case on this was decided very recently.

In *Barker v Lewis,* 2008 S.L.T. (Sh. Ct.) 17, there was a small rural development of five houses near St Andrews. The development was regulated by real burdens in a deed of conditions which included a restriction on the properties being used as a domestic dwelling house only. The proprietors of one house started using their house for a bed and breakfast business and the neighbours objected. In the appeal from the Sheriff's decision at first instance, the Sheriff Principal stated that material detriment must amount to substantial inconvenience or annoyance. This seems a higher standard than was the case under the common law which may not be what was intended in the Act. It may mean that neighbours are not guaranteed to show the requisite interest.

The final point to note on enforcement of real burdens is who is liable for the burdens? Affirmative burdens can only be enforced against the owner of the burdened property under s.9(1). Negative and ancillary burdens can also be enforced against a tenant or other occupier under s.9(2). If the burdened property is divided, all parts are liable for the burdens.

Variation and Discharge of Real Burdens

Under the common law, it was virtually impossible prior to 1970 to vary or discharge a real burden without the consent of the benefited proprietor who was often a superior. A variation of discharge was normally effected by a deed known as a minute of waiver, but payment was frequently demanded before a waiver was granted. This position was improved by the introduction of the Lands Tribunal for Scotland under the Conveyancing and Feudal Reform (Scotland) Act 1970. Part of the remit of this new tribunal is to hear applications from burdened proprietors to vary or discharge real burdens and other title conditions. The position under the

1970 Act and the reforms to this introduced by the Title Conditions (Scotland) Act 2003 are discussed below.

After the 2003 Act, it is still possible to agree a minute of waiver or to make application to the Lands Tribunal. In addition, new ways of varying or discharging a real burden are introduced. Statutory provision is made for a real burden to be extinguished where acquiescence or negative prescription has taken place. Acquiescence is a form of personal bar and applies when a real burden is breached without any objection by the person entitled to complain. Under the common law, a benefited proprietor could lose an interest to enforce a real burden by acquiescence.[93] The Act introduces a statutory rule on acquiescence for all real burdens which now exists along with the common law position. Section 16 provides that where a real burden is breached in a particular way, the burden is extinguished to the extent of the breach.

Various conditions must be satisfied. Material expenditure must be incurred by the burdened proprietor, the work involved must be obvious and the benefit of this expenditure would need to be lost if the burden was enforced. Once the work has been substantially completed, if there is no objection in a period of 12 weeks, there is a presumption that there was no objection. If one of the owners of a house in the cul-de-sac of seven houses already used as an example decides to build a conservatory which contravenes a community burden, this provision may operate if the other house owners in the cul-de-sac do not object. The house owner has incurred material expenditure on the conservatory and it is obvious to the others in the cul-de-sac that one is being built. The expenditure would be lost if the burden is enforced and the conservatory cannot be completed. After 12 weeks without objection, it will be presumed that the six house owners who did not object have consented. They will have acquiesced under the statutory provision in the Act.

Section 18 of the 2003 Act introduces a new negative prescription provision. If a real burden is breached without challenge for a period of five years, it is extinguished to the extent of the breach. In the case of the conservatory, no one could challenge its erection after five years.

Special provision is made for either variation or discharge of community burdens under the Act in ss.32–37. The reason for this is that a community may be large and the normal method of varying and discharging a real burden is by all proprietors concerned signing a minute of waiver. This may be impracticable in a large community. Section 33 allows for this to be done by a majority of the proprietors. There is protection provided for the minority who did not sign, as a copy of the deed and a notice must be sent to them and they have a right to object to the Lands Tribunal within eight weeks. In this case, the Tribunal will decide on whether the burden should be preserved, which it will do only if the variation or discharge is not in the best interests of the proprietors of all the properties in the community or is unfairly prejudicial to one or more of them. Registration of the deed which varies or discharges the burden requires a certificate obtained from the Lands Tribunal that no objections were received.

There is an alternative procedure under s.35 whereby the deed can be signed, not by the majority, but only by the owners of adjacent units within four metres of the burdened property. There are alternative provisions on giving notice. Notice can be sent to non-signing benefited owners, can be fixed to lamp posts in the vicinity or can be by advertisement in a local newspaper. The same provisions for objection apply.

One final provision introduced in the 2003 Act is informally referred to as the "sunset rule". This is to deal with very old burdens which no longer have any use or relevance and allows certain burdens to be extinguished. Sections 20–24 set out the procedure for this, in which the burdened proprietor is dramatically referred to as "the terminator". A real burden at least a hundred years old, except for conservation burdens, maritime burdens and family and service burdens can be discharged. Notice must be given to the benefited proprietors, along similar lines used for variation and discharge of community burdens, who have eight weeks to apply to the Lands Tribunal for renewal of the burden. If there is such application, the Lands Tribunal will decide on this. If there is no application, the notice of termination can be registered when certified by the Lands Tribunal that there is no such application. On registration, the burden is discharged.

Servitudes

A servitude is similar to a real burden and acts as a restriction on land ownership. It is a property right which allows a land owner to enter onto or make use of land belonging to a neighbour. As with real burdens, it is a real right which runs with the land. Like a real burden, a servitude must have both a burdened and a benefited property. Unlike a real burden, a servitude may exist without registration in the title. The most common type of servitude is a right of access or right of way whereby one property owner is allowed to cross part of a neighbour's property. Servitudes exist under the common law which derives from Roman law and has some similarities with the English law on easements. The Title Conditions (Scotland) Act 2003 makes important provisions in relation to servitudes, but they remain largely governed by the common law. One of the changes introduced in the 2003 Act is to re-categorise certain servitudes and real burdens. A servitude is defined by Bell as a "burden on land or houses, imposed by agreement, express or implied, in favour of the owners of other [land]".[94]

This makes it clear that there must be two properties involved, a benefited and a burdened property, and that a servitude can be express or implied. It is important to note that the terminology usually used in servitudes can be confusing. The burdened property is referred to as the "servient tenement" and the benefited property is referred to as the "dominant tenement."

Types of servitude
Before the 2003 Act came into force, servitudes could either be positive or negative and had to fall within a fixed list of known servitudes which had developed over time. The reason for this is that not all servitudes appear in

the title of the burdened proprietor and it would be unfair to someone who buys property to find that a previously unknown servitude affects the property.

The list of main servitudes includes:

- right of way or passage over the burdened land;
- *aquaeductus*, the right to run water over or under the burdened land;
- *aquaehaustus*, the right to draw water from a source in the burdened land;
- pasturage, the right to feed cattle or sheep on the burdened land;
- stillicide, the right to let water run from buildings onto to burdened land; and
- light and prospect which are negative servitudes which prevent building on the burdened land over a certain height or interfering with light or a view.

This list is not exhaustive but the list of known servitudes could not be expanded and in various cases attempts to do so failed. In *Mendelssohn v The Wee Pub Co Ltd*, 1991 G.W.D. 26–1518, a servitude of hanging a sign was not recognised and in *Neill v Scobbie*, 1993 G.W.D. 13–887, a servitude for overhead cables was similarly not recognised. A new servitude may be recognised if it is analogous to an existing one. In an interesting recent case, *Moncrieff v Jamieson*, 2008 S.C. (H.L.) 1, a servitude of parking was recognised after doubts on whether this exists.

It is clear that real burdens and servitudes are very similar and, in particular, negative servitudes are virtually identical in effect to negative real burdens. The opportunity was taken in the 2003 Act to simplify matters and re-categorise real burdens and servitudes. In ss.79–81, it is provided that it is no longer competent after November 28, 2004 to create a negative servitude. All existing negative servitudes are converted to negative real burdens and all existing real burdens which consist of a right to enter or otherwise use the burdened property are converted to positive servitudes. This makes the law on real burdens and servitudes under the common law and the Act clearer and more distinct.

One further point to note on the nature of servitudes before creation is examined, concerns the way in which servitudes are exercised. A servitude right is interpreted in the least restrictive way. It generally only requires inactivity on the part of the burdened proprietor. For example, if it is a right of way along a path, there is no duty to keep the path free from weeds or potholes. The burdened proprietor merely has to allow access to be exercised over the path. It is even permitted to have a gate across the path, as long as this is not locked. The benefited proprietor must exercise the right *civiliter*, which means that it must be exercised reasonably and in the least burdensome way. The benefited proprietor must not unreasonably increase the burden, such as using a servitude for pedestrian access as one for vehicles.

Creation of Servitudes

A servitude must be praedial, which means that there must be a benefited property and a burdened property and the servitude must not be for the personal benefit of the owner of the benefited property. There must be two separate properties that are the benefited and burdened property in separate ownership. These must be neighbouring properties. Normally, they will be contiguous, but this is not absolutely essential, provided that any distance between them does not completely diminish the benefit of the servitude. Prior to the 2003 Act coming into force, a servitude required to be a known servitude or analogous to a known servitude, but this requirement is specifically abolished under s.76 of the 2003 Act.

A servitude may be express or implied. Express servitudes can appear in a separate deed or can be created by express grant or express reservation in a disposition transferring ownership. An express grant is where the granter of the disposition, the disponer, gives a servitude to the grantee of the disposition, the disponee. Express reservation is where the disponer reserves a servitude right to himself when transferring the property to the disponee. It is possible, and not unusual, to have both an express grant and express reservation in the same disposition. Under the Requirements of Writing (Scotland) Act 1995 s.1(2)(b), a servitude created by express grant or reservation must be in writing and under s.75 of the 2003 Act it must be registered in the title of both the benefited and burdened property. Somewhat surprisingly, there is no need to use the term "servitude" in its creation, unlike the requirement to use the term "real burden" or specific type of real burden in the creation of real burdens.

It is possible for an implied servitude to be created. This can be by implied grant, where the benefited property is transferred, or by implied reservation, where the burdened property is transferred. The basis for this is that the need for the servitude was overlooked and the servitude is necessary for the reasonable enjoyment of the property. A servitude is more likely to be created by implied grant than by implied reservation. In *Ewart v Cochrane* (1869) 4 Macq. 117, the implied servitude sought was a right to use a certain drain leading from the Cochrane's tanyard to a cesspool on land belonging to Ewart. The House of Lords held that an implied servitude was essential for the enjoyment of the property. Conversely, in *Murray v Medley,* 1873 S.L.T. (Sh. Ct.) 75, the implied servitude sought was a right to use a water pipe which ran under a building and piece of land sold by Murray to Medley and serving both Medley's property and the property retained by Murray. The Sheriff held there was no implied servitude. It seems a surprising decision that piped water is not necessary for the comfortable enjoyment expected of a house.

An obvious example of a situation where an implied servitude should exist is in the case of a property which is landlocked. If someone sells part of his or her property and retains land which is completely surrounded by other land without reserving a right of access, there will be no way to get to the landlocked property. It would seem only fair that access should be legally possible somehow. This was the situation in *Bowers v Kennedy,* 2000 S.C. 555. The Inner House held in this case that the landlocked proprietor did have a right of access, but that this was an inherit right of landownership. It follows from this, that this right will continue and cannot be lost by prescription, unlike a servitude right whether express or implied.

The final way in which a servitude can be created is by prescription. A positive servitude can be created by prescription and used for a period of 20 years under the Prescription and Limitation (Scotland) Act 1973 s.3. The possession must be open, peaceable and without judicial interruption, as discussed in the section on Prescription above. The possession must be of such a nature that the use is being made as of right as opposed to use by permission or tolerance. Servitudes created by prescription can be difficult to establish.[95] They can create problems for conveyancers as they do not appear in the title deeds.

Extinction of Servitudes
A servitude can be extinguished in a number of ways. These are:

• express discharge;
• confusion;
• prescription;
• acquiescence;
• compulsory purchase; and
• Lands Tribunal.

An express discharge of a servitude must be in writing and the deed effecting the discharge must be registered in the title of the burdened property to be effective.[96] Confusion or *confusio* is where the burdened and benefited property come into the same ownership. The requirement for two separate properties in separate ownership is no longer fulfilled and the servitude disappears. If the two properties are separated again, the servitude must be recreated. This is not the position with real burdens.

Where a servitude is not exercised for the long negative prescription period of 20 years, the servitude will be extinguished.[97] It may be partially extinguished by prescription. If it is a right of way for vehicle and pedestrian traffic and it is not used for vehicles for over 20 years, the servitude for pedestrian traffic will continue.

Acquiescence operates as a form of personal bar, as noted in the section on Variation and discharge of real burdens above. If the benefited proprietor allows the burdened proprietor to take action which prevents the benefited proprietor exercising the servitude, the right to enforce may be lost. This is more likely if expenditure was incurred which would be lost if the servitude is enforced. If someone has granted a neighbour a right of access across the front of his or her garden and subsequently spends money on a pond and water feature which prevents the right of the access being exercised, without objection by the neighbour, acquiescence may occur.

If a property is compulsory purchased, any servitudes are extinguished.[98] The same applies to real burdens.

Finally, the Lands Tribunal is empowered to extinguish servitudes. This is discussed below.

Wayleaves and Public Rights of Way

Wayleaves are pipeline servitudes which are granted in favour of utility companies under various statutes. They allow the utility company, for example, Scottish Gas, to enter onto property to lay and maintain service pipes. The statutes contain various provisions regarding reinstatement of the ground and relative matters.

A public right of way is different from, but has similar effect to a servitude right of way. It is also different from the public access rights introduced under the Law Reform (Scotland) Act 2003, discussed above. Under the common law, a public right of way can be created to give members of the public a right of way from one public place to another. They can be over public or private land and can be created expressly, which is rare, or by positive prescription for 20 years.[99]

Public rights of way only require a burdened property, unlike servitudes which also require a benefited property. The right of way must be between two public places. It only allows access and does not confer other rights. As with servitudes, the use must be as of right and not by permission or tolerance. The public use must be substantial, must be continuous and uninterrupted and be exercised along the whole route. What is substantial use will depend on the nature of the right of way. The route may be in a populous area or in a remote one. The use may vary according to the season, for example, where it leads to a beach. There is a useful discussion on the requirements for a public right of way in *Cumbernauld & Kilsyth District Council v Dollar Land (Cumbernauld) Ltd,* 1993 S.C. (H.L.) 44, concerning a right of way through a shopping centre in Cumbernauld.

Like servitudes, public rights of way must be exercised in the least burdensome way to the landowner and they can be extinguished by prescription if not used for 20 years.[100]

Variation and extinction of title conditions

As already noted, it was not possible for a burdened proprietor to vary or discharge a real burden or other title condition prior to 1970 unless the benefited proprietor consented or had lost an interest to enforce this. When the Land Tribunal for Scotland was established under the Conveyancing and Feudal Reform (Scotland) Act 1970, the position for burdened proprietors improved. One of the functions of this new tribunal is to receive and adjudicate on applications to vary or discharge title conditions. Title conditions are defined to include real burdens, servitudes and conditions in registrable leases under s.122 of the 1970 Act. Certain conditions in favour of the Crown, relating to minerals and to agricultural holdings are excluded. The original provisions in the 1970 Act are replaced and updated in ss.90–104 of the Title Conditions (Scotland) Act 2003. Under s.90(1)(a), any owner of a benefited property or other person against whom a title condition is enforceable can apply to the tribunal to vary or discharge the title condition.

Under the 1970 Act there were three grounds on which a variation or discharge could be made. These were:

- a change in the character of the land rendering the obligation unreasonable or inappropriate;
- the obligation is unduly burdensome compared with any benefit resulting; and
- the existence of the obligation impedes some reasonable use of the land.

Under the 2003 Act s.98, the sole ground is now that the Lands Tribunal is satisfied that it is reasonable to grant the application having regard to 10 factors set out in s.100. These factors encompass the three grounds under the 1970 Act and include such other matters as a grant of planning permission has been made for a use which the title condition prevents and a catch-all of any other factor which the Lands Tribunal considers to be material. They are factors only and are taken into account in deciding whether the variation or discharge is reasonable.

When the Land Tribunal receives an application, it must be intimated to certain people, including the owner of the benefited property or the holder of a personal real burden. If the applicant is not the owner of the burdened property, it must be intimated to the owner. It may be intimated to others, such as a tenant. Applications in respect of community burdens can be made by owners of one quarter of the units in the community, and can be in respect of all or part only of the units in the community.[101] A period of 21 days is allowed for representations to be made. If unopposed, the application is normally granted automatically. This did not happen under the 1970 Act procedure and is a welcome improvement. If representations are made, the tribunal will consider the application and make its decision. A fee is payable if a representation is made, which was not required for objections under the 1970 Act procedure and this fact, plus the ability of the tribunal to award cases against an objector, helps avoid objections purely as a delaying tactic.

The Lands Tribunal has power to impose a new title condition which appears to be reasonable as a result of the variation or discharge. In this event, the applicant can either accept this or opt for the title condition to remain.[102] There are provisions for awarding compensation to the benefited proprietor for either substantial loss or disadvantage resulting from the variation or discharge, or to make up for any reduction in the consideration paid to the benefited proprietor due to the existence of the obligation.[103]

Finally, it can be noted that the Lands Tribunal has the power to decide on the validity, applicability, enforceability and interpretation of title conditions. This is a useful additional power under the 2003 Act[104] which enables an application to be made to the Lands Tribunal to decide such matters where there is some doubt as to the position.

---

[89] Bell, *Principles*, s.974.
[90] *RHM Bakeries (Scotland) Ltd v Strathclyde Regional Council*, 1985 S.L.T. 214.
[91] *Ross v Baird* (1827) 7 S. 361.
[92] 2003 Act s.1(1).
[93] *Ben Challum Ltd v Buchanan*, 1955 S.C. 348.
[94] Bell, *Principles*, s.979.

[95] See *Aberdeen Council v Wanchoo*, 2008 S.C. 278.
[96] 2003 Act s.78.
[97] Prescription & Limitation (Scotland) Act 1973 s.8.
[98] 2003 Act s.106.
[99] Prescription & Limitation (Scotland) Act 1973 s.3(3).
[100] Prescription & Limitation (Scotland) Act 1973 s.8.
[101] 2003 Act s.91.
[102] 2003 Act s.90(8) & (9).
[103] 2003 Act s.90(6).
[104] 2003 Act s.90(1)(a)(ii).

7. LEASES

A lease is a contract between a landlord, usually the owner, and a tenant to use or possess land or other heritable subjects for a certain period in return for a rent, usually money. It is an ancient legal concept and an old statute dating back to 1449 still in force.

There are three distinct types of leases. These are:

- residential leases;
- agricultural leases and crofts; and
- commercial and industrial leases.

Residential leases can be in either the public or private sector. Many people do not own their own home but live in houses which are owned by private owners or organisations such as local authorities or housing associations. Leases regulate various matters relating to tenants occupying these homes which they do not own. They form an important area of property law and there is considerable legislation controlling this area which is discussed below.

Agricultural leases and crofts are also subject to considerable statutory controls. An agricultural holding is a lease of land used for agriculture as part of a business. The statutes governing these are the Agricultural Holdings (Scotland) Acts 1991 and 2003. Crofts were established after the Highland Clearances and relate to small holdings of land in certain counties. The Land Court and Crofters Commission have important roles in the regulation of crofts and the principal statutes governing these are the Crofters (Scotland) Act 1993 and the Crofting Reform etc. (Scotland) Act 2007. Agricultural leases and crofts are a specialised area of law and further discussion is beyond the scope of this book.

Commercial and industrial leases are largely free from specific statutory control[105] and depend on the contractual terms of the lease. There is extensive case law relating to these, including various English cases which are helpful but must be treated with caution. Most commercial leases are full repairing and insuring leases which make the tenant solely liable for repairs. This is different from the common law position. Commercial leases are also a specialised area of law.

In all types of lease, the common law and general statutes on leases applies in addition to any specific legislation.

Essentials of a lease

With the exception of leases for less than one year, a lease must be in writing under the Requirements of Writing (Scotland) Act 1993. Until 2000, there was no limit on the length of a lease and these could be for as long as 999 years. Since 1974, it has not been possible to create a new residential lease for more than 20 years, and since 2000, a lease cannot be longer than 175 years. Longer leases existing prior to then remain valid.

There are four essentials for a contract of lease. These are:

- two separate parties;
- heritable subjects;
- a period; and
- a rent.

As a lease is a contract, the parties must agree on its terms and these parties must be two separate legal persons. It is not possible for a legal person to be both landlord and tenant. In *Kildrummy (Jersey) Ltd v Commissioners of Inland Revenue,* 1991 S.C.L.R. 498, a lease was held to be invalid as the tenant company was a trustee and nominee of the landlord and not a separate legal person.

The subjects must be heritable, otherwise the contract will be for hire not a lease. The subjects must be properly identified in the lease. It is possible to lease fishing rights or rights to shoot game separate from the land where the fish and game are situated.

The period of the lease must be definite or ascertainable. The period is known as the term and the end of the term is known as the ish. It cannot be for a period more than 175 years under s.67 of the Abolition of Feudal Tenure etc. (Scotland) Act 2000. The reason for this restriction being introduced in the Act which abolished feudalism was that there was a desire to prevent the possibility of "feudalism by the back door" whereby very long leases could be granted on conditions similar to feudal tenure. Residential leases cannot be for longer than 20 years under s.8 of the Land Tenure Reform (Scotland) Act 1974. Where there is agreement between the parties on all the essentials of a lease but no period has been specified, the law will imply a period of one year or a shorter period if consistent with the other terms of the lease.[106]

There must be a rent, which will normally be a sum of money paid periodically throughout the term of the lease. If there is no rent, there will be no lease but only a licence to occupy.

Real rights in leases and security of tenure

As a lease is a contract, at common law it is only personally binding and does not bind the successors of a landlord. This is unsatisfactory for the tenant as there is nothing to prevent the landlord selling to someone and the successor of the landlord ejecting the tenant. To remedy this defect, the Leases Act 1449 was introduced and is still on the statute book today. If the requirements of the Act are satisfied, the tenant in a lease has a real right which is enforceable against the landlord and the landlord's successors. The requirements of the Act are the four essentials for a lease already noted, plus two additional requirements. The tenant must have entered into possession of the leased premises, which can be natural or civil possession, and the title of the landlord must be registered.

The provisions under the Leases Act 1449 effectively now apply only to short leases. It is also possible to acquire a real right in a long lease, which is one for 20 years or more, by registration in the Register of Sasines or Land Register.[107]

The protection of obtaining a real right under the Leases Act 1449 or by registration of a lease ensures that a tenant will not be forced to vacate the subjects before the end of the term of the lease. In certain residential and agricultural leases there are statutory provisions to give tenants security of tenure beyond the end of the period of the lease.

An additional important principle in leases is that if no notice to quit is served by a landlord on a tenant before the end of the period of lease, the lease will renew for a period of one year or a shorter period if the original period was shorter than one year. This is under the principle of tacit relocation, discussed below.

Obligations of a landlord

A landlord has various obligations under a lease. These are:

* to give full possession for the full period of the lease;
* not to prejudice the possession;
* to provide the subjects in reasonable condition for their purpose; and
* to keep the subjects in repair.

Possession by the tenant is the whole purpose of a lease. The possession must be full possession and for the full period. A landlord cannot let a house with a room containing some belongings locked and unavailable to the tenant, unless this is agreed by the tenant.

Prejudicing the possession is where the landlord does something which adversely affects the tenant's use of the subjects of the lease. The obligation to refrain from doing this is sometimes referred to as the obligation not to derogate from the grant. Landlords must be careful to avoid actions which could amount to prejudicing the possession. In *Golden Sea Produce Ltd v Scottish Nuclear Plc,* 1992 S.L.T. 942, the owners of a fish hatchery business leased a site at Hunterston A Power Station for their business. The lease included a right to use the waste heated cooling water from the power station. A large stock of fish died from pollution by chlorine in the water pumped from the power station and used by the tenants. It was held that the landlords' actions were a contravention of the obligation not to do anything which adversely affected the tenants' operations under the lease.

This obligation is only in respect of a landlord's deliberate actings. In *Chevron Petroleum (UK) Ltd v Post Office,* 1987 S.L.T. 588, a basement leased by a tenant was flooded from their landlord's premises above, due to the negligence of the landlord's contractors. This was held not to be deliberate and not a breach of the landlord's obligation.

The subjects must be provided in a suitable condition for their use. An old case, *Kippen v Oppenheim* (1847) 10 D. 242 illustrates that a house must be habitable and not infested with cockroaches and bugs. If the subjects are let for commercial purposes, the landlord must provide these, but it is the responsibility of the tenant to ensure that the precise commercial use is possible and permitted, for instance, under planning legislation.[108]

The obligation to keep the property in repair means that if a lease is an urban as opposed to a rural lease, which is one which is not for agricultural purposes, a landlord must keep the subjects in a tenantable and habitable condition throughout the period. The property must be maintained in a wind and watertight condition. In *Gunn v National Coal Board,* 1982 S.L.T. 526, a tenant succeeded in a claim for damages due to a breach of the landlord's obligation, where rising damp had caused dampness and mould in a house. A landlord must be aware of the need for repair before there will be a liability and the obligation to repair does not apply where the damage is caused by *damnnum fatale,* such as a flood or hurricane, or by third parties.

The landlord's common law obligation of repair is supplemented by significant statutory provision in relation to residential leases which is discussed below.

Obligations of a tenant

A tenant also has various obligations under a lease. These are:

- to enter into possession and use and occupy the subjects;
- to use only for the purposes let;
- to take reasonable care of the subjects; and
- to pay the rent when due.

It is in the landlord's interest that the tenant actually occupies and uses the subjects for the period of the lease. The subjects may deteriorate otherwise. If a tenant does not, a landlord may rescind the lease for breach of contract. In *Blair Trust Co v Gilbert*, 1940 S.L.T. 322, the tenant in a lease of a farm was sent to prison for culpable homicide for three years and the landlord was entitled to rescind the lease for a breach of this obligation. In commercial leases, it is usual to insert what are known as "keep open" or "keep trading" clauses to ensure that the tenant continues to occupy and trade from the commercial premises and such clauses will be enforceable by the courts.[109]

A tenant cannot use the subjects for a different purpose than that agreed in the lease.[110] If the subjects are let for residential purposes, for example, they cannot be used as a business. If the tenant does use the subjects for a different purpose, this is sometimes referred to as inverting the possession. This obligation not to invert the possession also covers the obligation on a tenant not to make any alterations to the subjects without the landlord's consent.

A tenant must take reasonable care of the subjects. In *Mickel v McCoard,* 1913 S.C. 896, a tenant left a house for a period in winter and was held liable for damages caused by burst water pipes. The obligation continues until the lease comes to an end. In *Fry's Metals Ltd v Durastic Ltd,* 1991 S.L.T. 689, a tenant was held liable for damage caused when vandals broke into premises just before the end of a lease when the tenants had vacated, but before the keys were handed back to the landlord.

A tenant must pay the rent on time. If the lease is one to which a landlord's hypothec still applies, a tenant must plenish the subjects to secure the rent, which means that a tenant is obliged to stock the subjects with sufficient moveable property to be available as security for the rent. This is explained below.

Remedies for breach of terms of a lease

As a lease is a contract, both the landlord and tenant will have the usual contractual remedies available to them for breach of contract. These are:

- interdict;
- specific implement;
- recission if the breach is material; and
- damages.

In addition, a landlord will have the usual remedies of a creditor for recovery of debt if the tenant fails to pay the rent. This will include an action for debt using summary diligence where the lease has been registered in the Books of Council and Session.

A landlord also has a hypothec over certain moveable property in the leased subjects. Prior to the Bankruptcy and Diligence etc. (Scotland) Act 2007, this applied to all leases and was a useful remedy available to the landlord. It enabled the landlord to sell various moveable items belonging to the tenant in the leased premises, known as *invecta et illata.* This included furniture and stock-in-trade in a shop, but excluded money and clothing. It also included moveable property on the leased subjects that did not belong to the tenant. The hypothec enabled the landlord to sell these items to recover the rent but only the current year's rent and not arrears. Under the 2007 Act, a hypothec can no longer be used in residential and agriculture leases[111] and its remaining use for commercial leases has been updated.

A landlord may be able to irritate the lease. An irritancy means that the lease comes to a premature end and the tenant's rights are extinguished.

An irritancy can be legal or conventional. A legal irritancy is implied by law and occurs at common law if a tenant does not pay rent for two years. There are also legal irritancies in legislation on agricultural holdings and crofts.[112] A conventional irritancy is where the lease has a specific term allowing this to happen. Leases often have such a term. There are statutory controls on conventional irritancies. A landlord must give a tenant 14 days written notice before an irritancy can take place in respect of a breach of a monetary obligation, such as failure to pay the rent. In respect of breaches of a non-monetary obligation, a landlord may enforce an irritancy where in all the circumstances a fair and reasonable landlord would do so.[113]

A landlord cannot physically eject a tenant, even if the tenant is in breach of the terms and obligations under the lease. The landlord must raise an action of removing. This involves giving notice to the tenant that the action is to be raised.

In addition to the normal contractual remedies, a tenant may be entitled to retain the rent or to an abatement of the rent. Retention is where the rent is withheld due to a landlord being in breach of an obligation, for example, to repair the leased subjects. This is established in law, but there can be practical difficulties in exercising this. Once the landlord has remedied the breach, the retained rent must be released to the landlord.[114] Abatement of rent is where the rent is reduced because the tenant has been deprived of the use of the leased subjects to some extent, for example, where it has been uninhabitable for a certain period.[115]

Assignation and subletting

The general principle is that a tenant cannot assign a lease to a new tenant without the consent of the landlord. This is due to the operation of the doctrine *delectus persona,* meaning the landlord personally knows and accepts the particular tenant. The right to assign with consent is often inserted in a lease, but unless this is worded to say that consent will not be unreasonably withheld, a landlord will retain the right to accept or reject a particular new tenant.[116]

If an assignation does take place, the assignee is substituted for the original tenant and when the assignation is intimated to the landlord the original tenant ceases to have any rights or liabilities in respect of the lease.

Similarly, subletting is not possible unless the landlord agrees. Where it takes place, the original lease remains in force with all the rights and liabilities of the landlord and tenant intact and a new lease between the original tenant and the subtenant is created. There is no contractual relationship between the landlord and the subtenant unless the landlord is a party to the sublease.

Termination and tacit relocation

A lease will terminate in the following circumstances:

- at the ish or end of the period;
- irritancy;

- recission by the landlord or tenant;
- renunciation by both parties;
- total destruction of the subjects; or
- death of the tenant if granted for the tenant's lifetime.

A lease will not terminate automatically at the ish unless a notice to quit has been given by the landlord to the tenant before the end of the period. The period of notice may be agreed in the lease but there are minimum periods laid down by statute for particular types of lease.[117] If a landlord fails to give notice to quit, the lease will be renewed under the principle of tacit relocation for a further period of one year or if the original period was less than one year, for the same period.

It is essential that a landlord remembers to serve the appropriate notice or the tenant will be entitled to the benefit of tacit relocation. Equally, this can operate the other way. If a tenant does not want to run the risk of the lease continuing, notice to quit must be served.

If the leased subjects are totally destroyed, the principle known as *rei interitus* operates and the lease will come to an end.[118]

Residential Leases

Residential leases can be in either the public or private sector and, in addition to the common law rules and general legislation, there are extensive statutory provisions for both sectors. For a large part of the twentieth century, landlord and tenant legislation depended on the political views of the government of the day and there was a tendency for a new government to change the law to better fit its philosophy. The law became over complicated and confusing. The Rent Acts, as they were generally collectively known, were notorious. Towards the end of the century, the law was simplified and became more coherent, although it does remain fairly complex. An outline of this is given below.

Public sector

Following the Second World War there was a considerable growth in public sector housing and tenancies. This social housing was largely built by and leased out by local authorities as council housing, but towards the end of the century there was an increase in the number of tenancies available through housing associations. Ironically, public sector tenants did not have the same protections as private tenants and in 1980 substantial reform was introduced which included the right to buy at a discount. The law in public sector leases was recently consolidated under the Housing (Scotland) Act 2001. The Act introduced a new tenancy, the Scottish secure tenancy and all public sector tenancies are now Scottish secure tenancies or short Scottish secure tenancies.

Several conditions must be satisfied to qualify as a Scottish secure tenancy.[119] The landlord has to be one of a local authority, a registered social landlord (mainly housing associations) or a water or sewerage authority. The house must be let as a separate dwelling and the tenant must be an individual. The house must be the only or principal home of that individual. Certain categories of tenancy are specifically excluded under Sch.10 of the 2001 Act. There are 10 in total, including service tenancies, student lets and accommodation for homeless persons.

The key feature of the Scottish secure tenancy is security of tenure. A tenant has the right to continue to reside in the property regardless of any term expressed in the lease.[120] The tenant can give four weeks notice to terminate the lease,[121] but the landlord only has a limited power to end the tenancy. There are 15 grounds for recovery of possession by the landlord set out in Sch.2. Seven of these are conduct grounds and eight are management grounds. The landlord must give the tenant at least four weeks notice of the ground of termination and specify a date after which court proceedings will be raised for recovery of possession. Notice must also be given to qualifying occupiers of the property. If the tenant does not vacate the property, a summary cause action must be raised in the Sheriff Court.

The court can only grant an order for recovery of possession on one of the conduct or management grounds. The conduct grounds include such matters as rent arrears, deterioration in the condition of the property due to neglect by the tenant and antisocial conduct. The management grounds include such matters as overcrowding and the property is due to be demolished.

The rent under the tenancy is set by the landlord. The landlord has a statutory repairing obligation in addition to the common law obligation. The tenant has a right to a written lease and the right to buy property in certain circumstances.[122]

On the death of the tenant under a Scottish secure tenancy, the tenancy can pass to a qualified person.[123] On the death of the qualified person it can pass to a second qualified person, but no further when the second qualified person dies. There are a large number of possible qualified persons. These are:

- the tenant's spouse;
- the tenant's unmarried partner, heterosexual or same sex who resided there six months prior to the death;
- a member of the tenant's family which is broadly defined aged at least 16; and
- a carer of the tenant or member of the tenant's family who gave up their previous home.

A short Scottish secure tenancy is available in certain limited circumstances where a temporary tenancy only is appropriate, such as for a homeless person.[124] It gives no security of tenure to the tenant. It must be for a minimum of six months and the landlord must serve a notice on the prospective tenant confirming the type of tenancy before the tenancy commences. Although of very limited application, this tenancy is modelled on the short assured tenancy under the private sector.

Private sector

Under the private sector, the types of tenancy which have been used since 1989 are assured tenancies or short assured tenancies. Prior to 1989, private sector tenancies were regulated tenancies and prior to 1965 they were controlled tenancies. Assured tenancies and short assured tenancies are largely regulated by the Housing (Scotland) Act 1988, Pt II, which came into force in January 1989.

An assured tenancy requires a house to be leased as a separate dwelling and be occupied by the tenant as the tenant's only or principal home.[125] This includes a flat and can be part only of a house, so long as it is let as a separate dwelling. As with Scottish secure tenancies, there is a long list of 16 categories which are excluded from assured tenancies under Sch.4 of the 1988 Act. These include licensed premises or shops which include a house, student lets and where the landlord is resident in the same house.

Tenants under an assured tenancy have security of tenure. This is triggered when a landlord serves a notice to quit. Unless the tenant voluntarily vacates, the tenancy technically changes then from a contractual assured tenancy to a statutory assured tenancy with security of tenure. A tenant is able to give notice to quit of at least 28 days and vacate the premises.

A landlord under an assured tenancy can recover possession only by obtaining a court order in the case of one of the grounds listed in Sch.5 of the Act.[126] The grounds are not exactly the same as for Scottish secure tenancies. There are two categories of mandatory and discretionary grounds. If one of the mandatory grounds is established, the Sheriff must grant an order for possession and if one of the discretionary grounds is established, the Sheriff will only grant an order if satisfied that it is reasonable to do so.

The mandatory grounds include where the landlord formally occupied the house as the landlord's only or principal home and now requires the house for his or her own home or for his or her spouse, where there is default on a standard security granted before the tenancy and the creditor requires to sell the house with vacant possession and where the rent is three months in arrears. Discretionary grounds include where the rent is persistently late, where the house is deteriorating due to the tenant's neglect and where there is criminal or antisocial use by the tenant or someone visiting the house.

The rent is fixed by the landlord. The market place determines what will be a fair rent but there is fall back whereby a tenant can refer a notice of a rent increase to the Private Rented Housing Panel (formerly the Rent Assessment Committee) under s.25 of the Act, if the tenant feels that the new rent is above the proper market rent.

Under an assured tenancy, the tenant is entitled to a written lease.[127] There is an implied term that the tenant shall not assign or sublet the subjects in whole or in part without the consent of the landlord.[128] There are no provisions which correspond to the qualifying successor provisions in Scottish secure tenancies in the public sector. When the tenant dies the assured tenancy comes to an end.

The landlord's statutory obligation in relation to repairs was previously set out in Sch.10 of the Housing (Scotland) Act 1987. There is now a new statutory duty in relation to repairs, known as the Repairing Standard, which was introduced under the Housing (Scotland) Act 2006, Pt I which affects landlords under assured tenancies. This sets out details of the repairing standard required in private tenancies and includes provision that installations providing water, gas, electricity, heating and hot water must be in good working order. Tenants can apply to the Private Rented Housing Panel if they feel their landlord has failed to comply with the standard. This panel is empowered to refer the matter to the Private Rented Housing Committee which can issue a repairing standard enforcement order to the landlord. If the landlord does not comply, there are provisions to enable a local authority to undertake this work and recover the costs from the landlord. The Committee can also make a rent relief order which has the effect of reducing the rent until the landlord complies.

In addition to assured tenancies, the 1988 Act introduced short assured tenancies. These were necessary due to the security of tenure provisions in assured tenancies and have proved to be very popular with landlords who, understandably, do not want all their tenants to have security of tenure. A short assured tenancy does not give security of tenure and a landlord under such a tenancy has the right to recover possession at the end of the period in the lease.

To qualify as a short assured tenancy, the period must be at least six months and the prospective tenant must be given written notice in advance that the tenancy will be a short assured tenancy.[129] Provided the landlord gives two months notice to quit, the tenancy will end and the end of the period and a landlord can recover possession on the ground that the period has expired, in addition to the normal grounds for recovery of possession in assured tenancies.

In relation to leases in the private sector, there are further regulatory provisions which operate. Since 2000, where a landlord leases a house for multiple occupancy, such as to a number of students, under the Civil Government (Scotland) Act 1982 a landlord must obtain a multiple occupancy licence from the local authority. This is now required where the house is let to three or more persons. Before a licence will be issued, the local authority must be satisfied that the house complies with certain minimum standards of accommodation facilities, amenities and fire precautions.

Under the Antisocial Behaviour etc. (Scotland) Act 2004, Pt VIII, a new licensing system for compulsory registration of private landlords by local authorities has been introduced. A landlord must be a fit and proper person to act as a landlord and it is a criminal offence to let out a property without a licence.[130] The 2004 Act Pt VII also introduces provisions to tackle antisocial behaviour by tenants in the private sector. A local authority can serve an antisocial behaviour notice on a landlord if an occupant of tenanted property appears to be engaging in antisocial behaviour.[131] This is extended to include visitors to the house and there are various sanctions for failure to comply. These provisions make landlords potentially liable for all the activities of tenants and their visitors. It is not yet possible to gauge how workable these provisions are and how frequently they will be used by local authorities in practice.

[105] Exceptions are the Tenancy of Shops (Scotland) Act 1949 and 1964.
[106] *Gray v University of Edinburgh*, 1962 S.C. 157.
[107] Registration of Leases (Scotland) Act 1857, as amended by the Land Registration (Scotland) Act 1979.
[108] *Ballantyne v Meoni*, 1997 G.W.D. 29–1489.
[109] *Retail Parks Investment Ltd v Royal Bank of Scotland*, 1996 S.L.T. 669 and subsequent cases.
[110] *Bayley v Addison* (1801) 8 S.L.T. 379.
[111] Bankruptcy and Diligence etc. (Scotland) Act 2007 s.208(3).
[112] Agricultural Holdings (Scotland) Act 1991 s.20 and Crofters (Scotland) Act 1993 s.5.
[113] Law Reform (Miscellaneous Provisions) (Scotland) Act 1985 ss.4–7.
[114] *Pacitti v Manganiello*, 1995 S.C.L.R. 557.
[115] *Renfrew District Council v Gray*, 1987 S.L.T. (Sh. Ct.) 70.
[116] *Lousada & Co Ltd v J E Lessel (Properties) Ltd*, 1990 S.C. 178.
[117] For example, Sheriff Courts (Scotland) Act 1907.
[118] *Cantor Properties (Scotland) Ltd v Swears and Wells Ltd*, 1980 S.L.T. 165.
[119] 2001 Act s.11(i).
[120] 2001 Act s.14.
[121] 2001 Act s.12(1)(f).
[122] Housing (Scotland) Act 1987 ss.61–84, as amended by the Housing (Scotland) Act 2001.
[123] 2001 Act s.22.
[124] 2001 Act s.34.
[125] Housing (Scotland) Act 1988 s.12(i).
[126] 1988 Act s.18(i).
[127] 1988 Act s.30.
[128] 1988 Act s.23.
[129] 1988 Act s.32(i) and (ii).
[130] Antisocial Behaviour etc. (Scotland) Act 2004 s.93(i).
[131] 2004 Act s.68.

8. SECURITIES OVER HERITABLE PROPERTY

Lending institutions, such as banks and building societies, will not normally lend anything other than small sums without security. Usually this will be taken over the borrower's heritable property. Most people are not able to purchase a house outright and require a mortgage to help finance the purchase. If this is provided by a lender, it will be on the basis that the borrower grants a heritable security over the house to the lender as security for the mortgage. Heritable securities are also used as a matter of course in commerce.

A heritable security comprises two elements, a personal obligation and a security over the heritable property. The personal obligation binds the borrower to repay the full amount of the loan and means that the lender can go against all the assets of the borrower in the event of default. The security over the heritable property gives the lender a real right in security and a first charge over the heritable property. If default occurs, the lender will be empowered to sell the property and recover the amount of the loan from the proceeds before any other creditors.

The law on heritable securities was substantially modernised in the Conveyancing and Feudal Reform (Scotland) Act 1970. This Act replaced the previous forms of heritable security and introduced one form of heritable security for universal use in Scotland known as a standard security. The 1970 Act remains the applicable statutory provision on heritable securities. It was amended to a limited extent relating to residential properties only under the Mortgage Rights (Scotland) Act 2001. An important set of rules which affect the granting of mortgage finance is found in the Council of Mortgage Lenders Handbook. This sets out various conditions which apply to mortgages from its member institutions and solicitors acting for borrowers must be careful to pay particular attention to these.

Standard securities

A standard security under s.9 of the 1970 Act can be granted over an interest in land for security of a debt. The interest in land must be any interest in land which is capable of being owned or held as a separate interest and to which a title can be registered in the Register of Sasines or Land Register. Debt is defined to include an obligation to repay or pay a sum of money and an obligation *ad factum praestandum*, which is an obligation to do something. This means that a standard security can be granted for other matters, such as to build something, other than simply repaying a loan, although this is by far the most common use. A standard security can be granted for a fixed sum or for a future or fluctuating amount.

Standard securities can be granted by individuals, or other legal persons provided they have the requisite power to borrow and grant security over heritable property. Standard securities must be registered to effect a real right and in the case of companies this must also be in the Companies Register of Charges.

Form

A standard security must be in writing and the 1970 Act provides for two forms which are simply known as Form A and Form B. These are set out in Sch.2. Form A is used when the personal obligation is included in the standard security itself and Form B is used where the personal obligation is in a separate deed. The statutory style is very straightforward and in the normal house purchase situation the standard securities used by banks and building societies are printed forms with blanks to be filled in.

Part of the reason for this is that the 1970 Act sets out various standard conditions which are automatically incorporated into all standard securities.[132] These deal with the borrower or debtor's rights and obligations and the lender or creditor's powers. With the exception of the power of sale and foreclosure, these can be varied by agreement between the debtor and creditor.[133] In practice, some of these are commonly varied.

Ranking

If there is more than one security over the same heritable property, the question of ranking is relevant. It is not unusual for someone to borrow a sum of money from one lender and at a later date to borrow a further sum of money from a different lender, using the same heritable property as security. If the second lender is satisfied that there is sufficient security in the heritable property to agree to this, a second standard security in favour of the second lender will be registered. The question of ranking of the two securities then arises.

The general common law rule is that ranking depends on the date of registration of the security. A standard security registered earlier than another standard security has prior ranking. If the securities are registered on the same day, the ranking will be *pari passu*, or equal. If an earlier standard security secures future borrowing, a later standard security which is registered and intimated to the earlier security holder will limit the prior ranking to the amount advanced as at the date of intimation. The creditors and the debtor can adjust the ranking by agreement. This can be done in the standard securities themselves or in a separate ranking agreement.[134]

Assignation, Restriction and Discharge

A standard security may be assigned in whole or in part. This is done by an assignation which must be registered.[135] Both the creditor and debtor can assign. On the death of the debtor, the liability is heritable in the succession of the deceased debtor but if the heritable property which is the subject of the security when realised does not pay off the debt, the balance must be paid from the rest of the estate. On the death of the creditor, the right under a standard security is moveable, except in calculation of legal rights. If the debtor is sequestrated, the heritable subjects vest in the trustee, but the trustee can only sell with the consent of the creditor, unless sufficient money is obtained to settle all debts secured by heritable securities.

A part of the security subjects may be released from the heritable security.[136] If there is part payment, a form of partial discharge and deed of restriction is used. If there is no payment, a deed of restriction only is used.[137]

A standard security is extinguished by payment of the debt in full or performance of the obligation secured. It is normal for the security to be formally discharged by registering a discharge in the Register of Sasines or Land Register.[138]

Default

The 1970 Act sets out detailed rules on what happens if the debtor defaults. This may be for a variety of reasons and the default will usually be a failure to pay the installments of the loan payments when due. The default may be respect of other matters, such as failing to maintain the property.

At the time of writing, the economy is in a very poor state and Scotland, along with other countries, finds itself in a period of economic gloom. This means that many people are facing problems in paying their mortgages and many businesses are in financial difficulties. Enforcement of heritable securities on default is all too common at present. The strict rules set out in the 1970 Act are mitigated to a certain degree, in relation to residential mortgages, as a result of the Mortgage Rights (Scotland) Act 2001. This allows certain people in certain situations to request the court to delay the action available to creditors, which can ultimately lead to debtors losing their homes.

The 1970 Act sets out three situations where the debtor will be in default and provides for the remedies which the creditor will have in these default situations. The debtor will be in default where:

- a calling-up notice has been served but not complied with[139];
- the debtor has failed to comply with other requirements[140]; or
- the proprietor of the security subjects is insolvent.[141]

Where a debtor is in arrears of repayment of the loan and the creditor wishes to proceed to recover the debt, the creditor will usually start the process by serving a calling-up notice. There are rules regarding the form of the notice and service. The period of notice is two months. The debtor cannot object to the notice. On the expiry of the notice, the debtor is automatically held to be in default and the creditor can exercise any of the remedies under the Act.

A notice of default can be used as an alternative to a calling-up notice. This is commonly used where the debtor is not in arrears of repayment, but has contravened some other obligation, such as failing to maintain the property. If, for example, a debtor has suffered roof damage due to January gales and fails to repair the house for whatever reason, this will be a matter of concern to the lender. The house may deteriorate without the necessary repairs being done which could lead to a drop in the value of the house. This could affect the lender if the house has to be sold and it is in the interest of the lender to have the work carried out. Again, there are rules regarding the form of the notice and service. In this case, it is open to the debtor to object to the notice. The debtor may, for instance, dispute that the repairs are outstanding. If there is an objection, the Sheriff Court will adjudicate on this. The notice period is one month. If the default is not remedied, the creditor can exercise all the creditors' remedies, except entering into possession which requires application to the Court.

Where the proprietor of the security subjects becomes insolvent, the proprietor is automatically in default. In this case, the creditor must either use the calling-up notice or notice of default procedure or apply to the Court under s.24 to be granted the power to exercise the creditor's remedies. In practice, many lenders will use the s.24 procedure of applying to the court for the necessary powers in all cases where a debtor is in default, instead of using either the calling-up notice or notice of default procedures.

The remedies available to the creditor under the 1970 Act are:

- sale;
- entering into possession;
- carrying our repairs; and
- foreclosure.

In exercising the remedies, a creditor has a common law duty to act reasonably. A creditor can sell the security subjects under s.25 of the 1970 Act by private bargain or public roup, which is a type of auction. There is a duty to advertise the property and to take all reasonable steps to ensure that the sale price is the best that can be reasonably obtained. If this is done, the statutory obligation will be satisfied and the onus is on the debtor to show that the price obtained was not the best price. In *Dick v Clydesdale Bank,* 1991 S.C. 365, the debtor failed in an attempt to make the lender delay selling the security subjects, as the debtor expected the value to increase when a pending announcement about a new bypass route was made. The Inner House held that the Clydesdale Bank was entitled to sell when it felt appropriate, provided all reasonable steps were taken to get the best price which could be reasonably obtained at that time.

If a creditor enters into possession, this will allow the creditor to receive any rents and to lease the subjects for up to seven years, or longer with the consent of the Sheriff Court.[142] A creditor in possession may become subject to certain liabilities by being in possession, which would not have been the case as a security holder only.[143]

The right to carry out repairs and to enter on the security subjects to effect these is separate from the right to enter into possession.

The right to foreclosure may be an important one when the property market is depressed, as it is at the time of writing. If the security subjects have been exposed for sale by public roup at a price not exceeding the amount due under the security of the selling creditor and all prior and *pari passu* securities and no purchaser has been found, after two months the seller can apply to the Sheriff Court for a decree of foreclosure.[144] If decree is granted, an extract of this can be registered which will transfer the title to the property to the creditor. This will extinguish the debtor's right of redemption and will disburden the subjects of the foreclosing creditor's security and all postponed securities.

The Mortgage Rights (Scotland) Act 2001 was passed by the Scottish Parliament to mitigate the possible hardship to people who are in danger of losing their home due to financial difficulties of the debtor under a standard security. Certain people affected by the enforcement powers of the creditor can apply to the Sheriff Court for a suspension of enforcement procedures. The Act applies to standard securities over land used to any extent for residential purposes.[145] The persons who can use the provision are:

- the debtor;
- the proprietor who is not the debtor;
- the debtor or proprietor's non-entitled spouse;
- the debtor or proprietor's cohabitant, either heterosexual or same sex; and

- the debtor or proprietor's former cohabitant who continues to live in the security subjects with a child under 16 of the cohabitant and debtor or proprietor.

The proprietor who is not the debtor is intended to cover situations where the security is granted not by the debtor but a third party guarantor. The security subject must be wholly or partially a matrimonial home within the meaning of the Matrimonial Homes (Family Protection) (Scotland) Act 1981. In the first of the two cohabitant situations, the cohabitants must be living together as husband and wife or have all these characteristics other than the persons are of the same sex. In the second, the cohabitant must have lived with the debtor or proprietor for at least six months prior to the debtor or proprietor leaving. All these categories are intended to protect individuals who would be vulnerable if the debtor or proprietor deserts the security subjects used as a home.

An application for suspension of enforcement procedures can be made under s.11 of the 2001 Act where the creditor has taken steps to enforce the security by serving a calling-up notice or notice of default or by applying to the court under s.24. Where a calling-up notice has been served, the application must be made before the two month notice period has expired, and where a notice of default has been served it must be made not later than one month after the expiry of the one month notice period.

The court is given a wide discretion to determine the application. It is empowered under s.2(1) to suspend the enforcement of the security to an extent, for a period and subject to such conditions as it thinks fit, if it is reasonable in all the circumstances, having regard to four factors. These are:

- the nature and reason for the default;
- the applicant's ability to fulfil the obligation in default within a reasonable period;
- any action taken by the creditor to assist the debtor; and
- the ability of the applicant and any other person residing in the security subjects to secure reasonable alternative accommodation.

If an order is made, a certified copy is registered in the Register of Inhibitions. The Keeper will register the order against both parties and any other relevant party.

There is one final matter which may affect the creditor's ability to exercise the various remedies available on default by the debtor. This is in the situation where security is granted for business debts of a spouse over a house belonging to both spouses. It is essential in such a situation that the spouse who agrees that the house can be used as a security for a business debt receives separate legal advice regarding this. If this does not happen, the spouse may be able to have the security reduced in respect of his or her one half share. In a default situation, this will diminish the security available to the creditor.[146] In all situations where there is a third party or guarantor involved, separate legal advice should be obtained by the parties.

Floating charges

A floating charge is a security which can be created over heritable or moveable property by companies or limited liability partnerships. It is an English concept which was introduced into Scotland in 1961.[147]

A floating charge must be in writing and must be registered in the Companies Register of Charges within 21 days of creation.[148] It is not registered in the Register of Sasines or the Land Register. They are usually created over all the assets of the company, both heritable and moveable. This increases the security available to the creditor and floating charges are frequently used by lending institutions in loans to companies.

They operate very much as their name suggests. The charge does not attach to a company's assets initially but "floats" over the assets until a specific event occurs which causes the charge to crystallise and attach to all the assets of the company. This happens when the creditor takes action to enforce the security. This could be the appointment of an administrator or receiver or when the company goes into liquidation. Until such time, the charge is not a fixed charge. Any asset of the company which is sold is free of the charge. Conversely, any asset which the company acquires is subject to the floating charge. Floating charges are extinguished when the debt is paid in full.

Floating charges have been subject to much criticism since their introduction and reform is introduced under the Bankruptcy and Diligence etc. (Scotland) Act 2007. Once the provisions of the Act are fully in force, the most significant change will be that all floating charges must be registered in a new register, the Register of Floating Charges, to create the security[149].

---

[132] 1970 Act s.11(2) and Sch.3.
[133] 1970 Act s.11(3).
[134] 1970 Act s.13(3)(b).
[135] 1970 Act s.14 Sch.4.
[136] 1970 Act s.15.
[137] 1970 Act Sch.4.
[138] 1970 Act s.17 Sch.4.
[139] 1970 Act Sch.3, s.9(1)(a).
[140] 1970 Act Sch.3, s.9(1)(b).
[141] 1970 Act Sch.3, s.9(1)(c).
[142] 1970 Act Schs 3 and 10.
[143] *David Watson Property Management Ltd v Woolwich Equitable Building Society*, 1992 S.C. (H.L.) 21.
[144] 1970 Act s.28(1).
[145] 2001 Act s.1(1).
[146] *Smith v Bank of Scotland,* 1997 S.L.T. 910 and subsequent cases.
[147] Companies (Floating Charges) (Scotland) Act 1961.
[148] Companies Act 1985 ss.410 and 420.
[149] Bankruptcy and Diligence etc. (Scotland) Act 2007 ss.37–38.

9. CONVEYANCING AND A TYPICAL CONVEYANCING TRANSACTION

What is Conveyancing?

Property lawyers are often referred to as conveyancers and property law and conveyancing go hand in hand. What exactly is meant by the term "conveyancing"? It has been defined by Wood in his *Lectures in Conveyancing* (1903) as "the art which deals with the transfer of property in writing". Conveyancing is the process of preparing the documents which transfer rights. It is not confined to heritable property, but most work of conveyancers deals with heritable property. In its widest meaning conveyancing covers not just the actual drafting of documents, but also the technical and procedural rules connected with the transfer of property rights and the various practical ramifications of a particular transaction. Advising and guiding clients on these matters is an essential element of conveyancing.

A typical conveyancing transaction is the sale and purchase of a house, although it covers any matter in which a property right is transferred from one person to another. It includes, for example, the lease of a shop, taking out a mortgage from a lender to finance a commercial development or the transfer of property belonging to a deceased person to the beneficiaries. The law of property directly affects how conveyancing is conducted and the rules and procedures which must be followed in practice are detailed and complicated. It is not possible to cover all these within the scope of this book, but an outline of a typical conveyancing transaction, followed by an overview of some of the principles in practice involved, may be useful.

A typical conveyancing transaction

The following is an outline only, taking the common example of the sale and purchase of a house. There are various steps in this process:

- pre-contract;
- contract;
- examination of title and conveyancing;
- settlement; and
- registration.

Pre-Contract

Before the contract stage is reached, both the purchaser and seller have certain steps to take which are usually facilitated by their solicitors. The first step for someone who wishes to purchase a house is to sort out the finance, to establish how much can be afforded and the appropriate price range. This will usually be determined by the amount of the potential purchaser's savings and how much can be borrowed, taking account of his or her employment and income position and ongoing liabilities. Most people are unable to buy a house outright and a mortgage from a bank, building society or other lender will be required. This will be secured by the lender taking out a standard security over the house. It is very common for a solicitor to help arrange a suitable mortgage.

At the time of writing, the ability to obtain a mortgage, especially for first time buyers, has become much more difficult than in recent years. This is due to the severe economic downturn which has had a very significant effect on lending. This, in turn, has severely depressed the housing market.

It is usual for a seller to use the services of an agent to sell his or her house. This will frequently be done by a solicitor, although separate estate agents can be employed. The agent will make the necessary arrangements for marketing the property. A controversial new requirement was introduced on December 1, 2008. This is the Home Report. It is now essential that a Home Report is available to potential purchasers when a property is marketed for sale. This has three parts which are: a single survey of the property, including a valuation carried out by a chartered surveyor; an energy report; and a property questionnaire. At this stage, it is wise for the seller's solicitor to check the title of the sale property and initiate any enquiries relating to the property which may be required.

Contract

Once a house is on the market for sale, it is open to potential purchasers to make an offer to purchase the property. In Scotland, contracts for the sale and purchase of houses and other properties are almost always made by what are known as missives. Instead of drawing up a bilateral contract between the seller and purchaser when a sale is agreed, potential purchasers are free to make an offer for the house. This should be a formal offer from the purchaser's solicitor with detailed conditions of purchase included. If the offer is to be accepted, the seller's solicitor will issue a letter of acceptance. Usually, this acceptance will not be an outright acceptance, but will be subject to certain qualifications or conditions. This means that until both the seller and purchaser agree all the conditions, there is no concluded contract. Once all the conditions are agreed, the letters which pass between the purchaser's and seller's solicitors form the concluded contract and are referred to as the missives.

Prior to the introduction of Home Reports, a purchaser would often arrange a survey of the house to establish its value and the condition of the house, as it would not be sensible to buy a house without a survey. Alternatively, it is always open to a purchaser to make an offer on condition that a satisfactory survey is obtained, which condition must be satisfied before the contract is concluded.

One of the ideas behind the introduction of Home Reports was to avoid the necessity for the purchaser to instruct and pay for a survey by making a survey obtained by the seller available to all potential purchasers. This prevents a prospective purchaser having to pay for a survey over a house which is not successfully purchased. This might happen on a number of occasions. This laudable aim is not necessarily proving to be the reality in practice. A survey obtained by a seller may not be acceptable to a purchaser or to a purchaser's lender who is providing the finance. They may wish to obtain an independent survey. It is too early at present to judge whether Home Reports are a successful innovation.

A seller may or may not accept a particular offer from a potential purchaser. Frequently, if there are a number of potential purchasers who wish to make an offer for the property, a closing date is set by the seller. This means that all the offers have to be lodged by a specified time when they will be considered by the seller. A seller is not bound to accept the highest offer or, indeed, any offer.

Examination of title and conveyancing
When the contract is concluded, the examination of title and conveyancing stage takes place. Examination of title is the process whereby the purchaser's solicitor ensures that the title of the house is in order and the seller is able to transfer a good title to the purchaser. The seller's solicitor starts the process by sending the title deeds to the purchaser's solicitor for examination. The process itself will differ depending on whether the title is registered in the Register of Sasines or the Land Register. The seller's solicitor must be satisfied that everything is in order and may raise various queries with the selling solicitor which the selling solicitor will investigate and confirm.

At the same time, the seller's solicitor will prepare the legal document or deed which transfers the title to the house from the seller to the purchaser. This is known as a disposition and is the heart of a conveyancing transaction. The terms of the disposition may be straightforward or may require considerable conveyancing skills to prepare. The terms of this disposition are then approved by the seller's solicitor and the disposition is signed by the seller to be ready for delivery at settlement.

If the purchaser is obtaining a mortgage to finance the purchase, the purchaser's solicitor will usually act for the lender and prepare the necessary documentation required by the lender. This will involve preparing a standard security over the house which the purchaser signs. Once the seller's solicitor is satisfied that everything is in order with the title and the necessary documentation is prepared and signed, settlement can take place on the date agreed in the missives.

Settlement
Settlement is when the purchaser and seller implement their obligations under the missives to enable the transfer of the house to take place. The purchaser's solicitor hands over the purchase price of the house to the seller's solicitor. In exchange, the seller's solicitor hands over the keys of the house to enable the purchaser to take possession, and also hands over the disposition signed by the seller which transfers the title to the purchaser.

All this is done quite frequently within the office of the selling solicitor but can be done by post. Money transfers are usually done electronically.

Registration
Following settlement, the seller has received the proceeds of sale and the purchaser has received possession of the house and the document transferring the title. It is essential that the purchaser's solicitor registers the disposition transferring the title straight away. If there is a mortgage, the standard security by the purchaser in favour of the lender is registered at the same time. As discussed above, registration is essential to obtain a real right in heritable property and various problems could arise if registration is delayed, as happened in the *Sharp v Thomson* and *Burnett's Trustees v Grainger* cases.

Once all these steps have been taken, the sale and purchase of the house has been completed. This is a brief outline only of the process which is more detailed than set out here.

Aspects of Conveyancing

Capacity
As conveyancing involves the transfer of a property right from one legal person to another, it is essential that the person effecting the transfer has the capacity to do so. So far as individuals are concerned, this involves consideration of two matters, age and mental capacity. Generally, children under the age of 16 have no legal capacity to enter into a conveyancing transaction under the Age of Legal Capacity (Scotland) Act 1991. A child cannot buy or sell a house although, interestingly, a child over 12 has testamentary capacity and can make a will. A child aged 16 or over has full legal capacity and may buy or sell heritable property in his or her own name. Under the 1991 Act s.3, there is provision for any transaction entered into by a child between the ages of 16 and 18 which is deemed to be prejudicial, to be set aside by a court before the age of 21 is reached.

It is also essential that a person effecting the transfer has capacity in the sense of sufficient mental capacity. A person suffering from a mental disorder may not have the capacity to enter into a transaction.

Although capacity is required to transfer property, this is not the same as the capacity to own property. It is possible for a child under 16 to own heritable property but that child is not able to transfer this. A parent acting on their behalf has the capacity to enter into a transaction on their behalf. Similarly, if a person owns heritable property and develops a mental illness which prevents him or her having legal capacity to enter into a transaction, a guardian acting under a guardianship order can transact on his or her behalf.

A juristic person such as a company, partnership or unincorporated association has capacity to transact, but there may be limitations on the capacity of such organisations under the constitution of the organisation or under statute. It is more accurate to say that the organisation has the capacity but lacks a power to do something. For instance, a company will have the capacity to make an offer for land and to take all necessary conveyancing steps in relation to that land, but may lack the power in its memorandum and articles to own that particular type of land, for example, agricultural land.

Authentication

A document or deed used in a conveyancing transaction must be in the correct form and correctly signed to be valid. The law on this was simplified in 1995 under the Requirements of Writing (Scotland) Act 1995. A deed which relates to a contract in respect of an interest in land or to a transfer of an interest in land must be in writing.[150] This simple rule means that all conveyancing deeds must be in writing. They must also be correctly signed.

Under the 1995 Act s.2, a deed is valid if it is signed by the person granting the deed, the granter. Nothing else is required for validity. This contrasts with the position prior to 1995 when it was usually the position that witnessing of the deed was required before the deed was valid. Witnessing does remain important after the 1995 Act. If a deed is properly witnessed, it is said to be probative. This means that it is self-proving and is presumed to be formally valid. This makes it less easy to challenge and conveyancers rely on probative deeds.

For individuals, a deed is probative if it is signed by the granter in the presence of one witness. There are separate rules about who must sign as the granter on behalf of companies, partnerships and other juristic persons to make the deed probative. In some situations a witness is required and in others a witness is not.

Deeds used in most conveyancing transactions are signed by the granter on the last page only and not on every page. Any plan or schedule annexed must also be signed by the granter. The granter subscribes, that is signs at the end. Only the sovereign superscribes, that is signs at the top. The witness must be aged 16 or over, have sufficient mental capacity and know the granter, even if he or she has just been introduced to the granter. The witness signs on the last page also, having seen the granter sign or acknowledge his or her signature. This must be done as part of a continuous process and not done at a later time.[151] The witness must be designed which means that the witness's name and address are given in the deed. This is usually set out in what is known as the testing clause which appears at the end of the deed and narrates the designation of the witness and the date and place of signing.

Missives—Contracts for sale and purchase

As noted above, it is usual for the contract stage in a conveyancing transaction to be completed by the use of missives. This stage has become increasingly more complex in recent years and is often the stage where most work on the part of solicitors takes place, with solicitors acting for the purchaser and seller negotiating to and fro on behalf of their clients before the contract is concluded. It is often said that the missives stage, whereby a binding contract for the sale and purchase is concluded quickly, is one of the strengths of the Scottish system of buying and selling. This is in contrast to the system of buying and selling in England where sales and purchases are usually not binding but "subject to contract" for a long period, due to a chain of interdependent transactions. This leads to uncertainty as to if and when a sale or purchase will go ahead. In recent years this traditional strength of the Scottish system has been undermined by missives taking longer and longer to be concluded.

The usual practice is for the missives stage to be initiated by the purchaser's solicitor making an offer to the seller's estate agent who may or may not be the seller's solicitor. There is nothing to prevent a person from making an offer personally, without using a solicitor as an agent. This is very unwise due to the complicated nature of contracts for the sale and purchase of a house. Where new houses which have just been built are being sold, it is more usual for the missives stage to be initiated by the builder's agent issuing an offer to sell. In either case, the offer will be a letter with detailed conditions which must be accepted before a contract can be concluded.

This type of contract for the sale and purchase of heritable property is governed by the general law of contract. The common law makes various provisions for this type of contract and there is little legislation which specifically affects such contracts, apart from the Contracts (Scotland) Act 1997 which is a very short statute.

A typical offer to purchase a house from a solicitor will run to several pages and contain around 20 clauses with detailed conditions. The provisions of many of the clauses are implied under the common law, but it is standard practice to include them in an offer. The only two essentials, strictly speaking, are the subject of sale and the price.

A typical offer will start by detailing the purchaser, the subjects of sale, the price and the date of entry, which is the settlement date. Care must be taken by the solicitor taking instructions on these and on all other clauses, as the solicitor is acting as agent for the potential purchaser and must be accurate in ascertaining the precise terms of the offer to be made. It is particularly important to check what is included in the sale as part of the purchase price. Most sellers will be including various items as part of the sale, such as carpets, white goods and garden sheds, but this will vary from seller to seller. The purchaser's solicitor must check what items the purchaser wishes to be included in the price offered.

Certain items will be included automatically as fixtures but, as discussed above, it is not always certain whether an item is a fixture and therefore heritable and deemed to be part of the house. To make the position completely clear, there will usually be a fixtures and fittings clause which will be a detailed list of the items included in the price, which are or may be moveable items and which the seller would otherwise be entitled to remove.

A typical offer will then include a clause detailing what will happen if settlement is delayed for any reason. This covers such matters as interest being payable on the price if it is late and when a seller can rescind the contract and resell the property if the purchaser fails to pay the price.

Detailed clauses are included in a typical offer relating to title matters and planning and development. Although it is an implied condition that a good marketable title will be given by the seller to the purchaser, a clause to this effect is invariably included. It will ensure also that there are no unusual or onerous burdens contained in the title to the property. Provision is made for the seller to produce various searches which are evidence that the title is in order. Provision is also made to confirm that the seller will grant a valid disposition transferring a good title to the purchaser.

The purchaser needs to know various matters relating to planning and development to ensure there is no problem with the house which he or she wishes to purchase or anything adverse is planned. For instance, a purchaser needs to know that any extension to the house was done properly after obtaining the necessary planning permission and building warrant. Similarly, a purchaser will want to know if a supermarket is planned for the grassy area opposite the front of the house. Such matters are covered by these clauses. Other technical clauses are included in an offer to protect the position of the purchaser.

All solicitors' firms have their own style of a typical offer which starts the missives stage. It might be thought that a standard offer is appropriate and that all offers should have the same clauses. It has not been possible to get the legal profession to agree to this, although this has been attempted in the past by the Law Society of Scotland. There are certain peculiarities in certain areas which have prevented this. What has happened is that firms of solicitors in certain parts of Scotland have been able to get together to agree to use a standard form within their own areas. There are Tayside Standard Missives which are used by solicitors in Tayside, Aberdeen Standard Missives used in Aberdeen and so on.

Once the offer is made, the seller has the option to accept or reject the offer. If it is to be accepted, it is possible to simply accept all the conditions and give an outright acceptance which is called a *de plano* acceptance. This is unusual as there are usually some qualifications to the offer which need to be made. These may be technical matters relating to the title or some other matter, or personal matters, such as the exclusion of certain items included in the price or a change in the proposed date of entry. Usually, a qualified acceptance of the offer will be made by the seller's solicitor.

As the acceptance is qualified, there is no consensus between the parties and the contract is not concluded. It will remain unconcluded until all the conditions are agreed by both parties. It may be that a qualification in the acceptance is not agreed by the purchaser and an alternative is suggested. Letters continue to pass between the purchaser's and seller's solicitors as the negotiation takes place and these form part of the missives until final agreement is reached. All of these letters which pass between the parties' solicitors then form the concluded missives, which is the concluded contract. Once this has happened, the terms of the missives are binding on the parties and the examination of title and conveyancing phase takes place. One further matter on missives which is useful to note is what happens if one party fails to implement their side of the contract?

A purchaser is obliged under the missives to pay the full purchase price on the agreed settlement date. If this is not done, the missives will provide for this situation. It is standard practice that the seller cannot immediately rescind the contract and resell the subjects. If a purchaser is due to pay the price on Friday May 31 and does not do so, it is not possible for the seller to sell to someone else on Monday June 3. The missives will, typically, first provide for interest to be paid on the unpaid price from the agreed date of entry. They will then provide that if the purchase price plus interest is not paid by a certain date, usually 14 days after the date of entry, the seller can give notice that he or she is intending to rescind from the contract after a reasonable period. Again this is usually 14 days. After the second period has elapsed without payment, the seller is free to resell and sue the purchaser for any loss made on the resale plus the expenses of resale. As an alternative, it is open to the seller to raise an action of implement against the purchaser, but this may well be useless if the purchaser does not have sufficient money to pay and this is the reason for not going ahead with the purchase. When it comes to resale, the seller is under a duty to obtain the best price possible which is the normal contract rule that a person who has suffered a breach of contract has a duty to mitigate their loss.

A seller has the duty under the missives to sell the house to the purchaser at the agreed price. A good marketable title must be given and if this cannot be given, the purchaser will rescind from the contract. If the seller refuses to sell to the purchaser for whatever reason, the purchaser can raise an action for implement, but it would be very unusual for a seller to simply refuse to sell after missives have been concluded. If the seller breaches any of the terms of the missives, for instance, by removing items which were included in the sale, the purchaser can retain the house and sue for damages for the non-inclusion of these items. This is known as the *action quanti minoris*, and one of the provisions in the Contract (Scotland) Act 1997 was to provide that such actions are lawful in Scotland.

Examination of Title and Conveyancing
After the missives are concluded, the purchaser's solicitor receives the title deeds from the seller's solicitor and proceeds to examine the title of the seller to ensure that the purchaser will receive a good marketable title. The purchaser's solicitor also proceeds to prepare the disposition, which is the conveyancing deed which transfers the title from the seller to the purchaser. Examination of the title is exactly what it says. The title of the seller is examined by the purchaser's solicitor to check everything is in order. This process is more straightforward where the title of the seller is registered in the Land Register as opposed to the Register of Sasines. The transfer of a property which is registered in the Land Register from the owner to a purchaser is known as a dealing.

If the seller's title is registered in the Land Register, the seller's title is guaranteed, which is the fundamental principle of registration of title in Scotland. Provided there is no exclusion of indemnity, the title of the seller which appears in the Land Register is not open to challenge. There is no need to look further back than the seller's title. What must be examined is the seller's title from the date of registration until the date of sale. This is to ensure that no adverse matter has taken place, such as the seller selling the property or any part of it to someone else, and to check whether any new standard securities have been granted over the property.

This process is facilitated by the seller's solicitor instructing search reports, approved by the purchaser's solicitor, against the title of the seller which will reveal any transactions registered in the title. Searches are also instructed against the seller as an individual to ensure that there is nothing which prevents the seller from granting a title. For instance, if the seller has an inhibition against him or her due to a pending court action, the seller cannot grant a valid title. At this stage the purchaser's solicitor will also examine the actual title certificate to confirm a variety of matters, which include checking what the seller owns corresponds with what has been offered for in the missives, establishing the terms of the burdens and servitudes affecting the property are not unduly burdensome or onerous and ascertaining any heritable securities which have been granted over the subjects which need to be discharged before settlement.

If the title of the seller is in the Register of Sasines, the transfer to the purchaser is known as a first registration because the disposition in favour of the purchaser must be registered in the Land Register for the first time. Although the object is the same, the purchaser's solicitor will need to examine more deeds to ensure that the seller has a good title to sell. This involves utilising the principle of prescription, as discussed above. The seller needs to show that there is a valid prescriptive progress in the title. This is likely to involve the purchaser's solicitor examining several, or possibly many, title deeds. The searches instructed in a first registration may also be more complex, although they serve the same purpose of demonstrating that there is a good marketable title which the seller can validly transfer to the purchaser.

Conveyancing and Dispositions

At the same time as examining the title and raising any questions on this which the seller's solicitor will need to answer before the settlement can proceed, the purchaser's solicitor prepares the disposition, which is the conveyancing deed which transfers the title from the seller to the purchaser and is registered in the Land Register. A draft of this is prepared which is sent to the seller's solicitor for approval and, once approved, the principal deed is drawn up. This is then signed by the seller and is ready to be handed over at settlement along with the keys, in exchange for the purchase price. The disposition is a unilateral deed. It is only signed by the seller and not by the purchaser.

The terms of the disposition depend on whether the seller's title is in the Land Register or the Register of Sasines. If it is in the Land Register, the terms are very straightforward and the document is short. This was one of the aims of introducing the Land Register. It was intended to make conveyancing simpler and less costly. If it is in the Register of Sasines, the terms of the disposition are more complex and a greater degree of skill in conveyancing is required.

A disposition which is used in a first registration will normally have the following clauses:

- narrative;
- dispositive;
- burdens;
- entry;
- warrandice; and
- testing clause.

The narrative clause describes the parties to the deed and narrates the circumstances of the transfer which will usually be a sale. Both the granter of the deed, the disponer, and the grantee of the deed, the disponee are detailed, although the deed is a unilateral deed and will only be signed by the granter, as noted above. Both the disponer and disponee must be designed. The disponer's designation must link up with the designation in the previous disposition in the disponer's favour which has been registered in the Register of Sasines and constitutes the existing title. If the disponer is granting the disposition in a capacity other than as an individual, for example, as a trustee, this will be narrated.

The dispositive clause is the key clause in the disposition which contains some words of conveyance signifying that the title is being transferred from the disponer to the disponee. The standard form of words used is "Do Hereby Dispone". The dispositive clause then gives a description of the property which in standard practice commences with the words "All and Whole". The description of the property must accurately describe the property and distinctively identify what is being conveyed or transferred. A good conveyancer will be well-skilled in this, but unfortunately not all descriptions in dispositions are accurate and unambiguous. This is compounded by the fact that not all dispositions contain a plan. Many older dispositions do not. The poor quality of descriptions in titles and the frequent lack of a plan were influential factors in the moves to introduce the new system of land registration which culminated in the Land Registration (Scotland) Act 1979.

There are three types of description which are general, particular and by reference. A general description simply describes the subjects by name, such as "North Vane Farm, Perthshire", without any reference to its physical boundaries. This type of description was fairly common at one time but is not adequate for a modern disposition. One of the two other types is appropriate, and which one is used depends on whether the property is being conveyed as it stands for the first time or has been conveyed previously.

If a property is being conveyed for the first time, a particular description is appropriate. This is a new description which will not have been used before. The property will be identified, usually using a plan, and the actual physical boundaries of the property will be described, preferably with measurements. If properly worded, the description should accurately and unambiguously identify exactly what is being conveyed in the disposition.

If the property is not being conveyed for the first time, there will be a particular description of the property in one of the dispositions which form part of the continuous title to the property. If a builder erected some houses in 2001 and sold a house to Mr Anderson that year and Mr Anderson sold the house to Mr Brown in 2008 and Mr Brown is now selling the house to Mr Christie, there will be a particular description of the house in the disposition conveying the house from the builder to Mr Anderson in 2001. In the disposition conveying the house from Mr Anderson to Mr Brown and from Mr Brown to Mr Christie, this particular description need not be repeated, although there is nothing invalid about doing so. Instead, a shorter description by reference can be used. This description simply refers to the fuller description in the earlier disposition. There is statutory authorisation of this under the Conveyancing (Scotland) Act 1924 s.8 and Sch.D. A valid description by reference must state the county for registration purposes in which the property is situated, specify the deed which is referred to for the description and that deed must contain a particular description.

The next clause in a disposition is the burdens clause. This will specify details of any new burdens which are being created or refer to existing burdens. To refer to existing burdens, all that is required is to give appropriate details of the deed or deeds where they are fully detailed. If new burdens are being created, the rules regarding these, discussed above, must be followed and care in drafting is required.

The burdens clause is followed by the date of entry which is the settlement date agreed by the parties when the disponee gains possession. Next comes the warrandice clause which follows on from the obligation to give a good marketable title in the missives. This represents a personal guarantee by the disponer that the disponer will indemnify the disponee against any loss or damage in value of the disponee's real right if there is complete or partial eviction from the property. This guarantee exists where absolute warrandice is granted which is usual, unless the property is being gifted or the disponer is granting other than as an individual.

Finally, the testing clause narrates the details of the execution of the deed once signed. There may be other clauses in addition to the foregoing which are appropriate in certain circumstances dealing with such matters as stamp duty land tax.

---

[150] 1995 Act s.1(2).
[151] *Walker v Whitwell*, 1916 S.C. (H.L.) 75.

BIBLIOGRAPHY

Brand, D., Steven, A. & Wortley, S. (eds), *Professor McDonald's Conveyancing Manual*, 7th edn (Edinburgh: Tottel, 2004).

Carey Miller, *Corporeal Moveables in Scots Law*, 2nd edn (Edinburgh: W.Green, 2005).

Cusine, D. & Rennie, R., *Standard Securities*, 2nd edn (Edinburgh: Tottel, 2002).

Cusine, D. & Rennie, R., *Missives*, 2nd edn (Butterworths/Law Society of Scotland, 1999).

Gloag & Henderson, *The Law of Scotland*, 12th edn (Edinburgh: W.Green, 2007).

Gordon, W., *Scottish Land Law*, 3rd edn (Edinburgh: W.Green, 2009).

Gretton, G. & Reid, K., *Conveyancing*, 3rd edn (Edinburgh: W.Green, 2004).

Gretton, G. & Steven, A., *Property, Trusts and Succession* (Edinburgh: Tottel, 2009).

Guthrie, T.G., *Scottish Property Law*, 2nd edn (Edinburgh: Tottel, 2004).

McAllister, A., *Scottish Law of Leases*, 3rd edn (Butterworths, 2002).

Paisley, R., *Land Law* (Edinburgh: W.Green, 2000).

Reid, *The Law of Property in Scotland* (Butterworths/Law Society of Scotland, 1996).

Rennie (ed.), *The Promised Land: Property Law Reform* (Edinburgh: W.Green, 2008).

INDEX

Abandoned property
acquisition of corporeal moveable
property, 12–13
Abatement of rent
tenants' rights, 68
Acceptance
conveyancing, 86
Access rights to land
landownership, 42–43
Accession
classification of property, 5
corporeal moveable property, 13
Acquiescence
real burdens, 56
servitudes, 60
Acquisition
corporeal moveable property
accession, 13
commixtion, 14–15
confusion, 14–15
derivative acquisitions, 15–16
generally, 10
occupation, 11–13
specification, 13–14
Action of removing
tenancies, 68
Action *quanti minoris*
conveyancing, 87
Actual delivery
corporeal moveable property
derivative acquisition, 15
pledges, 22
Ad factum praestandum
standard securities, 74
Affirmative burdens
real burdens
enforcement, 55
types of, 50
Age
capacity for conveyancing, 83
Agents
commercial agents
liens, 22
Agricultural holdings
landownership
fixtures, 33

Agricultural leases
hypothecs, 23
use of, 63
Airspace
encroachment, 32–33
landownership, 38
Alimentary liferents
see **Liferents**
Alluvion
landownership
rivers, 33
Ancillary burdens
real burdens
enforcement, 55
Antisocial behaviour
private sector tenants, 72–73
Aquaeductus
servitudes, 58
Aquaehaustus
servitudes, 58
Assignment
incorporeal moveable property
rights in security, 23
transfer of title, 17–18
leases
assured tenancies, 71
generally, 68
standard securities, 75
Assured tenancies
leases, 71–72
Authentication
conveyancing, 84
Avulsion
landownership
rivers, 33

Bad faith
possession, and, 6–7
Bona vacantia
acquisition of corporeal moveable
property, 13
Bonds in respondentia
hypothecs, 23
Bonds of bottomry
hypothecs, 23

Boundaries
  landownership, 32–33
Burdens
  conveyancing, 90
  land certificates, 27

Calling-up notices
  default of standard securities, 76
Capacity
  conveyancing, 83–84
Charges
  land certificates, 27
Civil partners
  occupancy rights, 10
Civil possession
  incidents of landownership, 41
  scope of, 6
Closing date
  conveyancing, 82
Clubs
  capacity for conveyancing, 83
  joint property, 8
Coal
  landownership
    physical extent, 33
    right of support, 43
Coelo usque ad centrum
  landownership, 32
Cohabitation
  occupancy rights, 10
Commercial agents
  liens, 22
Commercial leases
  hypothecs, 23
  use of, 63–64
Commixtion
  corporeal moveable property, 14–15
Common interest
  tenements
    generally, 9
    Tenement Management
      Schemes, 39
Common property
  co-ownership, and, 8
Community burdens
  types of real burdens, 50–51
Companies
  capacity for conveyancing, 83
Compulsory purchase
  extinction of servitudes, 60
Confusion
  corporeal moveable property, 14–15
  servitudes, 60
Conservation burdens
  types of real burdens, 50
Constructive delivery
  corporeal moveable property

  derivative acquisition, 15–16
  pledges, 22
Conveyancing
  acceptance, 86
  action *quanti minoris*, 87
  authentication, 84
  burdens clause, 90
  capacity, 83–84
  closing dates, 82
  date of entry, 90
  description of property, 89
  dispositions, 88–90
  examination of title
    generally, 87–88
    typical transaction, 82
  Home Reports, 81–82
  meaning, 80
  missives
    contents, 84–87
    typical transaction, 81
  offers, 84–86
  signatures
    authentication, 84
    testing clause, 90
  standard securities, 82
  surveys, 81–82
  testing clause, 90
  typical transaction
    contract, 81–82
    examination of title, 82
    pre-contract, 80–81
    registration, 83
    settlement, 82–83
  warrandice clause, 90
Co-ownership
  see also **Ownership**
  common interest, 9
  common property, 8
  joint property, 8
  pro-indiviso ownership, 8
Copyright
  intellectual property rights, 18–19
Corporeal moveable property
  acquisition, 10
  derivative acquisition, 10, 15–16
  original acquisition
    accession, 13
    commixtion, 14–15
    confusion, 14–15
    occupation, 11–13
    specification, 13–14
  rights in security
    floating charges, 23
    hypothecs, 23
    liens, 22–23
    pawnbroking, 22
    pledges, 21–22

transfers, 15–16
Corporeal property
    see also **Corporeal moveable
        property; Incorporeal
        property**
    incorporeal property, distinction
        from, 5
Creation
    personal rights, 7
    real burdens, 51–53
    real rights, 7
    servitudes, 59–60
Crops
    classification of property, 4–5
Crown
    corporeal moveable property
        wild animals, 11
        treasure trove, 12, 13
    landownership
        feudalism, 25
        restrictions on, 35–36
        water rights, 44

Delectus persona
    assignment of leases, 68
    transfer of incorporeal moveable
        property, 17
Delivery
    corporeal moveable property
        derivative acquisition, 15–16
        pledges, 22
Derivative acquisition
    corporeal moveable property, 10,
        15–16
Descriptions
    landownership
        conveyancing, 89
        physical extent, 32–33
        registration, 26–27
Designs
    intellectual property rights, 18
Destination
    classification of property, 5
Discharge
    real burdens, 55–57
    servitudes, 60
    standard securities, 75
Dispositions
    conveyancing, 88–90
Dominium
    meaning, 3
Dominium directum
    landownership, 24
Dominium eminens
    landownership, 25
Dominium utile
    landownership, 24–25

Ejection, rights of
    tenancies, 68
Encroachment
    landownership
        physical extent of, 32–33
        scope of, 41–42
Enforcement
    landlords' repairing obligations, 72
    personal rights, 7
    real burdens
        community burdens, 50
        conservation burdens, 50
        generally, 53–55
    real rights, 7
    suspension of
        default of standard securities, 78
Entry date
    conveyancing, 90
Entry into possession
    default of standard securities, 77
Examination of title
    conveyancing
        generally, 87–88
        typical transaction, 82
Exclusive possession
    landownership, 40–41
Express servitudes
    see also **Servitudes**
    creation, 59
Extinction
    public rights of way, 61
    servitudes, 60
    title conditions, 61–62

Facility burdens
    types of real burdens, 51
Fee
    liferents, 9
Feudalism
    landownership
        generally, 24–25
        real burdens, 49–50
Feuduties
    abolition of, 25–26
Fishing rights
    landownership
        Crown rights, 36
        incidents of, 45
        positive prescription, 31
Fixtures
    landownership
        functional subordination, 34
        generally, 33–34
        intention, 35
        permanency, 34–35
        physical attachment, 34

Floating charges
rights in security
corporeal moveable property, 23
heritable property, 79
Foreclosure
default of standard securities, 77
Foreshore
see also **Lochs; Rivers; Seabed**
landownership
Crown rights, 36
positive prescription, 31
Full repairing and insuring leases
use of, 64
Fungible property
see also **Non-fungible property**
nature of, 5

Game rights
landownership, 45
Gas
see **Natural gas**
Good faith
positive prescription, 31
possession, and, 6–7
Gratuitous alienation
landownership, 29
Guarantors
default of standard securities, 78

Health and safety
exclusive possession of land, 41
Heritable property
see also **Moveable property**
nature of, 4–5
securities over
floating charges, 79
generally, 73–74
standard securities, 74–78
HMO licences
requirements for, 72
Home Reports
conveyancing, 81–82
Hoteliers
liens, 22
Houses in multiple occupation
licences, 72
Hypothecs
landlords' rights, 23, 67
Human rights
positive prescription, 32
property law, and, 2

Illegality
real burdens, 52
Implied rights
enforcement of real burdens, 53–55

Implied servitudes
see also **Servitudes**
creation, 59
Improper liferents
see **Liferents**
Incorporeal moveable property
see also **Corporeal moveable property**
intellectual property rights
copyright, 18–19
designs, 20
patents, 18
trade marks, 19–20
rights in security, 23
transfer of title, 17–18
Incorporeal property
see also **Corporeal property; Incorporeal moveable property**
corporeal property, distinction from, 5
Industrial leases
use of, 63–64
Infringement
intellectual property rights, 19
Insolvency
landownership
registration, 29–30
Insurance
full repairing and insuring leases, 64
Intangible property
see also **Tangible property**
intellectual property rights
copyright, 18–19
designs, 20
patents, 18
trade marks, 19–20
nature of, 5
transfer of title, 17–18
Intellectual property rights
copyright, 18–19
designs, 20
patents, 18
rights in security, 23
trade marks, 19–20
Intention
corporeal moveable property
acquisition by occupation, 11
derivative acquisition, 15
landownership
fixtures, 35
possession, and, 6
real burdens, 52
Intimation
incorporeal moveable property
rights in security, 23
transfer of title, 17–18

ranking of standard securities, 75
Invecta et illata
landlord's hypothec, 67
Irritancy
abolition of, 25–26
leases, 67–68

Joint property
co-ownership, and, 8
Jura in re aleiena
meaning, 3
Jura in re propria
meaning, 3
Jus quesitum tertio
enforcement of real burdens, 54

Land certificates
landownership
registration, 27
Land Register
conveyancing
dispositions, 88
examination of title, 82, 87–88
floating charges, 79
landownership
boundaries, 32–33
registration, 26
standard securities
creation, 74
discharge, 75
Landlords obligations
generally, 65–66
repairing obligations, 72
Landownership
see also **Ownership**
extent of
Crown rights, 35–36
fixtures, 33–35
physical extent, 32–33
tenements, 36–40
historical background
feudalism, 24–25
feuduties, 25–26
irritancy, 25–26
incidents of
encroachment, 41–42
exclusive possession, 40–41
fishing rights, 45
game rights, 45
nuisance, 45
public access rights, 42–43
right of support, 43–44
trespass, 41–42
water rights, 44–45
prescription
negative prescription, 30
positive prescription, 30–32

registration
descriptions of land, 26–27
insolvency, 29–30
land certificates, 27
Land Register, 26
overriding interests, 28
rectification, 28–29
Register of Sasines, 26
restrictions on
extinction of title conditions,
61–62
generally, 46–47
nuisance, 47–48
public rights of way, 61
real burdens, 48–57
servitudes, 57–60
spite, 48
statutory restrictions, 48
variation of title conditions, 61–
62
wayleaves, 61
Tenement Management Schemes
common interest, 39
introduction of, 37
ownership of parts, 37–39
repairs, 39–40
Lands Tribunal
real burdens, 56
servitudes, 60
title conditions, 61–62
Latent trusts
transfer of title, 18
Law reform
property law, 1–2
Leases
antisocial behaviour, 72–73
assignment
assured tenancies, 71
generally, 68
assured tenancies, 71–72
breach, remedies for, 67–68
ejection, 68
essentials for, 64
HMO licences, 72
hypothec, 23, 67
irritancy, 67–68
landlords' obligations, 65–66
landownership
positive prescription, 31
unregistered leases, 28
parties, 64
period, 64
real rights, 65
recovery of possession
assured tenancies, 71
secure tenancies, 70
short assured tenancies, 72

remedies for breach, 67–68
removing, action of, 68
rent
    abatement, 68
    assured tenancies, 71
    requirement for, 64
    retention, 68
    secure tenancies, 70
repairing obligations
    assured tenancies, 72
residential leases
    assured tenancies, 71–72
    generally, 63
    hypothecs, 23, 67
    private sector, 70–73
    public sector, 69–70
    secure tenancies, 69–70
    short assured tenancies, 72–73
    short secure tenancies, 70
right to buy
    secure tenancies, 69
secure tenancies, 69–70
security of tenure
    generally, 65
short assured tenancies, 72–73
short secure tenancies, 70
subjects, 64
subletting
    assured tenancies, 71
    generally, 68
succession
    secure tenancies, 70
tacit relocation, 68–69
tenants' obligations, 65–66
termination, 68–69
types
    agricultural leases, 63
    commercial or industrial leases,
        63–64
    full repairing and insuring
        leases, 64
    residential leases, 63
Legal rights
succession to property, 4
Liens
rights in security
    corporeal moveable property,
        22–23
Liferents
property rights, 9
Light
servitudes, 58
Lochs
see also **Foreshore; Rivers; Seabed**
landownership, 44

Lost property
landownership
    Crown rights, 12, 36

Matrimonial homes
default of standard securities, 78
Mental disorder
capacity for conveyancing, 83
Missives
conveyancing
    contents, 84–87
    typical transaction, 81
Monopolies
real burdens, 52
Moveable property
see also **Heritable property**
corporeal moveable property
    accession, 13
    acquisition, 10
    commixtion, 14–15
    confusion, 14–15
    derivative acquisition, 15–16
    occupation, 11–13
    original acquisition, 10–15
    rights in security, 21–23
    specification, 13–14
    transfers, 15–16
incorporeal property
    copyright, 18–19
    designs, 20
    intellectual property rights, 18–
        20
    patents, 18
    rights in security, 23
    trade marks, 19–20
    transfer of title, 17–18
nature of, 4–5
rights in security
    corporeal moveable property,
        21–23
    floating charges, 23
    generally, 20–21
    hypothecs, 23
    incorporeal moveable property,
        23
    liens, 22–23
    pawnbroking, 22
    pledges, 21–22

Natural gas
landownership
    Crown rights, 33, 36
Natural possession
incidents of landownership, 40–41
scope of, 6

Negative burdens
real burdens
enforcement, 55
types of, 50
Negative prescription
landownership, 30
public rights of way, 61
real burdens, 56
servitudes, 60
Negative servitudes
real burdens, and, 58
Neighbour burdens
types of real burdens, 51
Nemo dat quod non habet
transfer of title
corporeal moveable property, 15
Non domino dispositions
positive prescription, 31
Non-fungible property
see also **Fungible property**
nature of, 5
Notices of default
default of standard securities, 76
Nuisance
landownership
incidental rights, 45
restrictions on, 47–48

Occupation
corporeal moveable property, 11–13
Occupiers liability
trespassers, 41
Offers
conveyancing, 84–86
Outer space
landownership
physical extent, 33
Overriding interests
landownership
registration, 28
Ownership
co-ownership
common interest, 9
common property, 8
joint property, 8
pro-indiviso ownership, 8
landownership
see also **Landownership**
extent of, 32–40
historical background, 24–26
incidents of, 40–45
prescription, 30–32
registration, 26–30
possession, distinction from, 6–7
property rights, 3

Pari passu
ranking of standard securities, 75
Partnerships
capacity for conveyancing, 83
Pasturage
servitudes, 58
Patents
intellectual property rights, 18
Patrimonial interests
enforcement of real burdens, 55
Pawnbroking
rights in security
corporeal moveable property, 22
Personal burdens
types of real burdens, 50
Pertinents
landownership
tenements, 38–39
Petroleum
landownership
Crown rights, 33, 36
Pipeline servitudes
wayleaves, 61
Pledges
rights in security
corporeal moveable property,
21–22
Pollution control
water rights, 44
Positive prescription
landownership, 30–32
public rights of way, 61
servitudes, 60
Possession
default of standard securities, 77
ownership, distinction from, 6–7
recovery of
assured tenancies, 71
secure tenancies, 70
short assured tenancies, 72
Praedial
real burdens, 50, 52
servitudes, 59
Precious metals
landownership
Crown rights, 33, 36
Prescription
landownership, 30–32
public rights of way, 61
servitudes
creation, 60
extinction, 60
Primogeniture
succession to property, 4
Private landlords
registration, 72

Pro-indiviso **ownership**
  common property, 8
Property
  classification
    corporeal, 5
    fungible, 5
    heritable, 4–5
    incorporeal, 5
    moveable, 4–5
    non-fungible, 5
    ownership, 6–7
    possession, 6–7
  meaning, 2–3
Property law
  human rights, and, 2
  law reform, 1–2
  nature of, 1
Property rights
  common interest, 9
  generally, 3
  liferents, 9
  occupancy rights, 9–10
  personal rights, 7
  real rights, 7
Prospect
  servitudes, 58
Public access rights
  landownership, 42–43
Public policy
  real burdens, 52
Public rights of way
  landownership
    positive prescription, 31, 61
  title conditions, 61

Quod nullius est fit primi occupantis
  acquisition of corporeal moveable
    property, 11

Ranking
  standard securities, 75
Real burdens
  abolition of feudal tenure, 49–50
  creation, 51–53
  discharge, 55–57
  enforcement, 53–55
  generally, 48–49
  interpretation, 52
  negative servitudes, and, 58
  types
    affirmative burdens, 50
    community burdens, 50–51
    conservation burdens, 50
    facility burdens, 51
    feudal burdens, 49–50
    negative burdens, 50
    neighbour burdens, 51

    non-feudal burdens, 49–50
    personal burdens, 50
    praedial burdens, 50
    service burdens, 51
  variation, 55–57
Real rights
  leases, 65
Receiverships
  landownership, 30
Recovery of possession
  assured tenancies, 71
  secure tenancies, 70
  short assured tenancies, 72
Rectification
  landownership
    registration, 28–29
Reddendo
  landownership, 24
Regalia
  see **Crown**
Register of Charges
  floating charges, 79
Register of Inhibitions
  default of standard securities, 78
Register of Sasines
  conveyancing
    dispositions, 88
    examination of title, 82, 87–88
  floating charges, 79
  landownership
    boundaries, 32–33
    positive prescription, 31
    registration, 26
  standard securities
    creation, 74
    discharge, 75
Registration
  conveyancing, 83
  designs, 20
  landownership
    descriptions of land, 26–27
    insolvency, 29–30
    land certificates, 27
    Land Register, 26
    overriding interests, 28
    rectification, 28–29
    Register of Sasines, 26
  private landlords, 72
  standard securities
    generally, 74
    ranking, 75
Rei interitus
  destruction of lease subjects, 69
Removing, action of
  tenancies, 68
Rent
  abatement, 68

assured tenancies, 71
requirement for, 64
retention, 68
secure tenancies, 70
Repairs
default of standard securities, 77
repairing obligations
assured tenancies, 72
full repairing and insuring
leases, 64
Tenement Management Schemes,
39–40
Res
meaning, 3
Res nullius
acquisition of corporeal moveable
property, 11–12
Residential leases
assured tenancies, 71–72
generally, 63
hypothecs, 23, 67
private sector, 70–73
public sector, 69–70
secure tenancies, 69–70
short assured tenancies, 72–73
short secure tenancies, 70
Restitution
recovery of possession, and, 7
Retention of rent
tenants' rights, 68
Retention of title
corporeal moveable property
derivative acquisition, 16
Right of support
landownership, 43–44
Right to buy
secure tenancies, 69
Right to light
servitudes, 58
Right to roam
public access to land, 42–43
Rights in security
corporeal moveable property
floating charges, 23
hypothecs, 23
liens, 22–23
pawnbroking, 22
pledges, 21–22
generally, 20–21
heritable property
floating charges, 79
generally, 73–74
standard securities, 74–78
incorporeal moveable property, 23
Rights of passage
servitudes, 58

Rights of way
landownership
positive prescription, 31
servitudes, 58
title conditions, 61
Riparian owners
water rights
navigable rivers, 44–45
non-navigable rivers, 45
Rivers
see also **Foreshore; Lochs; Seabed**
common interest, 9
landownership
Crown rights, 36
physical extent, 33
water rights, 44–45
Roaming rights
public access to land, 42–43

Sale of goods
derivative acquisition, 16
Sale of land
default of standard securities, 77
Salmon fishing
landownership
Crown rights, 36
positive prescription, 31
Scottish Outdoor Access Code
public access to land, 42–43
Seabed
see also **Foreshore; Lochs, Rivers**
Crown rights, 35–36
Secure tenancies
requirements for, 69–70
Security, rights in
corporeal moveable property
floating charges, 23
hypothecs, 23
liens, 22–23
pawnbroking, 22
pledges, 21–22
generally, 20–21
heritable property
floating charges, 79
generally, 73–74
standard securities, 74–78
incorporeal moveable property, 23
Security of tenure
assured tenancies, 71–72
generally, 65
secure tenancies, 69–70
short assured tenancies, 72–73
short secure tenancies, 70
Service burdens
types of real burdens, 51
Servitudes
landownership

positive prescription, 31
registration, 28
title conditions
creation, 59–60
extinction, 60
generally, 57
types, 57–58
Settlement
conveyancing, 82–83
Ships
hypothecs, 23
Short assured tenancies
requirements for, 72–73
Short secure tenancies
requirements for, 70
Signatures
conveyancing
authentication, 84
testing clause, 90
Solicitors
liens, 22
Solum
landownership, 38
Space, outer
landownership
physical extent, 33
Specification
corporeal moveable property, 13–14
Spite
landownership, restrictions on, 48
Spouses
non-entitled spouses
enforcement of real burdens, 54
occupancy rights, 9–10
succession
common property, 8
legal rights, 4
Spuilzie
recovery of possession, and, 7
Squatting
possession, and, 6
Standard securities
assignment, 75
conveyancing, 82
default, 75–78
discharge, 75
form, 74–75
introduction, 74
ranking, 75
restriction, 75
Statutory restrictions
landownership, 48
Stillicide
servitudes, 58
Subletting
assured tenancies, 71
generally, 68

Succession
classification of property, 4–5
common property, 8
legal rights, 4
primogeniture, 4
secure tenancies, 70
Sunset rule
real burdens
variation or discharge, 56
Support, right of
landownership, 43–44
Surveys
conveyancing, 81–82
Symbolic delivery
corporeal moveable property
derivative acquisition, 16
pledges, 22

Tacit relocation
leases, 68–69
Tangible property
see also **Intangible property**
corporeal moveable property
accession, 13
acquisition, 10
commixtion, 14–15
confusion, 14–15
derivative acquisitions, 15–16
occupation, 11–13
original acquisition, 10–15
specification, 13–14
transfers, 15–16
nature of, 5
Tenants' obligations
leases, 65–66
Tenants rights
enforcement of real burdens, 54
Tenements
common interest
generally, 9
Tenement Management
Schemes, 39
common property, 8
landownership
generally, 36–40
physical extent, 33
Tenement Management Schemes
common interest, 39
introduction of, 37
ownership of parts, 37–39
repairs, 39–40
Termination
leases, 68–69
Testing clause
conveyancing, 90
Theft
possession, and, 6

Tidal rivers
  see **Rivers**
Title conditions
  extinction, 61–62
  generally, 46–47
  public rights of way, 61
  real burdens, 48–57
  servitudes, 57–60
  variation, 61–62
  wayleaves, 61
Trade marks
  intellectual property rights, 19–20
Transfer of title
  corporeal moveable property, 15–16
  incorporeal moveable property, 17–18
Treasure trove
  Crown rights, 12–13, 36
Trees
  classification of property, 4
Trespass
  landownership, 41–42
Trusts
  latent trusts
    transfer of title, 18
  trust property
    joint property, 8

Unincorporated associations
  capacity for conveyancing, 83
  joint property, 8
Unregistered designs
  intellectual property rights, 20
Utilities
  wayleaves, 61

Variation
  real burdens, 55–57
  title conditions, 61–62

Warrandice clause
  conveyancing, 90
Water rights
  landownership, 44–45
  servitudes
    aquaeductus, 58
    aquaehaustus, 58
    stillicide, 58
Wayleaves
  title conditions 61
Wild animals
  acquisition of corporeal moveable
    property, 11–12